485

BRAZIL:
A Giant Stirs

by RICHARD P. MOMSEN, JR.

**Instituto Interamericano
de Ciencias Agrícolas de OEA**

A SEARCHLIGHT ORIGINAL
under the general editorship of

G. ETZEL PEARCY **GEORGE W. HOFFMAN**

The Geographer **Professor of Geography**
U. S. Department of State **University of Texas**

D. VAN NOSTRAND COMPANY, INC.
PRINCETON, NEW JERSEY

TORONTO LONDON
MELBOURNE

VAN NOSTRAND REGIONAL OFFICES
New York, Chicago, San Francisco

D. VAN NOSTRAND COMPANY, LTD., *London*

D. VAN NOSTRAND COMPANY (Canada), LTD., *Toronto*

D. VAN NOSTRAND AUSTRALIA PTY. LTD., *Melbourne*

Library of Congress Catalog Card No. 68–29172

Preface

Brazil is among the largest, most populous, and most diverse of nations. Sophisticated industrial products flow in profusion from the factories of its leading cities. Huge crop surpluses are produced on mechanized and efficient farms. Yet communities in the backlands barely subsist by farming, stock raising, or gathering forest products. Beside isolated beaches, somnolent villages depend upon the uncertain catches of fishermen whose dugout canoes and balsa rafts ply the lagoons or coastal waters. High on the rim of a nearly empty interior, yet only a few hours' flying time from most of the major cities, is Brazil's new capital and the world's most modern metropolis, Brasília. Here exotic skyscrapers overlook adobe huts, while business tycoons and international statesmen are carried to and fro by screaming jet over the heads of shoeless *caboclos,* who plod through the scrub beside creaking oxcarts.

Although most of Brazil is located within the tropics, it is a land of great physical variety. Furthermore, despite an overall cultural homogeneity and the common thread of historical and political unity, it is a country of disparate socio-economic expressions. These are now undergoing kaleidoscopic changes as Brazil moves away from its role as a semi-colonial exporter of unprocessed raw materials toward that of a modern urban-industrial society. Many of the country's most pressing problems spring from the effects of the quickening pace of this change on long-standing institutions.

The stresses and strains of modernization, as well as its benefits, are distributed very unevenly among Brazil's various regions. Differentiated into virtually discrete entities as a result of the long-term interaction between evolving occupancy patterns and the physical environment, the regional distinctions within Brazil are, and for most of its history have been, quite clearly defined. Each region is larger than most of the countries of Latin America, and each exhibits fundamentally different characteristics as to natural

3

resources, productivity, income structures, population densitie social differentiation, and political development. It is the regio which must, perforce, provide the basis for any meaningful analysi of the Brazilian milieu. The focus of this book is therefore upo these regions and the way they have developed through the variou stages of Brazil's growth as a nation.

As it would take many volumes to do complete justice to s varied and complex a country as Brazil, a selection of facts an themes is obligatory. For this reason, the manner of characterizin each region must differ. For one, the emphasis may be upon th physical environment and the processes of settlement. For anothe perhaps current social and economic values are more important Any apparent lack of topical consistency is the result of choosing from a great range of material, only that which is most pertinen to the salient geographic features of each region. The cumulativ effect should be to impart something of the elusive and ephemera spark which sets the Brazilians apart from other peoples, and ha welded them into a nation that is greater by far than the mere sun of its parts.

A final word about the brief list of suggested readings. This is in tended both for those who want to further their factual knowledg of this multi-faceted country, perhaps in more specialized fields and for those who wish to read more about Brazil for their own pleasure or broadened understanding. The list therefore include items of personal narrative (John dos Pasos and Carolina Maria d Jesus) and fiction (Jorge Amado) as well as recent substantiv works on special topics. The real fascination of Brazil lies, in th end, not so much in the straightforward facts of its physical en vironment, its history, or its political and economic institutions distinct and flavorful as these may be, but rather in the spirit o the Brazilians and the unique national culture they have evolvec within their own sizable share of the world's tropical lands. Ar understanding of this society is of added contemporary importance as Brazil stands on the threshold of a new era, in which she can b expected to exercise an ever widening influence in world affairs

A Brazilian story has it that when Saint Peter congratulated God upon the magnificent job he had done in creating the land that was to become Brazil, the Lord replied: "Just wait until you see the people who will be living there!" To this day, no happier combination can be found anywhere on earth.

RICHARD P. MOMSEN, JR.

Contents

Tables

Maps (following page 72)

A Giant Nation

Sᴛʀᴇᴛᴄʜɪɴɢ 2,700 miles from east to west and 2,500 miles north-south, Brazil is the world's fifth largest country. More extensive than the conterminous United States, it includes roughly one-half of the South American land mass, 3½ million square miles, and borders on every nation of that continent except Chile and Ecuador. Its 85 million people make it eighth in the world in population.

For so large a country, Brazil is singularly lacking in nature's extremes: it has no rainless deserts, no Arctic wastes, and no high mountains. Instead, the country derives an overpowering identity from the sheer vastness of its landscapes. In very few parts of Brazil does man not seem the perpetual intruder.

Through two million square miles of equatorial rain forest, numberless rivers unroll with only a rare ripple to mark man's fleeting use of their waters. Thousands of years of human occupancy have left scarcely a scar upon the endless jungle horizons of Amazonia, which extend to the very doorsteps of its largest cities, broken only occasionally by a solitary settlement.

Slicing diagonally across the Brazilian heartland for 2,000 miles is an interminable plateau, a dun-colored land of coarse grasses and stunted scrub, cut by tenuous trails leading off in the ill-defined distance to lonely ranches. A jumbled belt of harsh, corrugated mountains—thinly occupied by a scant populace that picks inconsequentially at the soil in search of mineral wealth or a simple subsistence crop—separates the plateau from the sea. And much of

Brazil's four thousand miles of shoreline is nearly as empty as the interior (Map 4). Between widely spaced port cities, with their well-peopled surroundings, forgotten settlements lie tucked away below craggy headlands or beside remote beaches, scarcely altered since the Portuguese first occupied these coasts.

Overwhelmed by the land that stretches endlessly around him, the average Brazilian, city dweller and backlander alike, regards the unfamiliar parts of his country with much the same emotion as he might the distant darkness of Africa or the incomprehensible glitter of North America about which, thanks to the cinema, he may well know more than he does about his own nation. Sheer distance and, until very recently, an appalling transportation system have tended to isolate the Brazilian within a few miles of his birthplace. This he seldom leaves by choice, although necessity and adventurism have sometimes driven him, generally as part of a band or migratory group, over unimaginable distances on incredible pioneering ventures.

From the general isolation imparted by this spatial superabundance, Brazil has become divided into distinct and traditionally recognized regions: the North, the Northeast, the East, the West, and the South (Map 1). We shall return to these in later chapters. But let us first look more closely at the principal natural features of Brazil, the better to understand this vast stage upon which that nation's human drama has unfolded.

THE LAND

Despite its size, a high proportion of Brazil's land area lies within the humid tropics (Map 5), and the outlines of its principal landforms can be drawn with bold and simple strokes (Map 2). There are three major landform regions in Brazil: the Amazon Lowland, the Central Highlands, and the Coastal Lowlands. There are also three smaller, peripheral ones: the Rio Grande do Sul Plains, the Pantanal, and the Guiana Highlands.

The last-named region is a rugged upland located along the borders of the Guianas and Venezuela. It attains 9,888 feet elevation at the Pico de Neblina, Brazil's highest point. Between the western rim of the Guiana Highlands and the Andes, the natural Casiquiari Canal, navigable by canoe, links the Orinoco River with the Rio Negro, the principal northern confluent of the Amazon.

The Amazon Lowland. In contrast to the only partly explored Guiana Highlands, the main valley of the Amazon has been well traveled since its first explorer, Francisco de Orellana, started down the Rio Napo in what is now Ecuador and reached its mouth in 1541—141 years before LaSalle made his voyage down the Mississippi. Today, ocean-going steamers call regularly at Manaus (Map 3), nearly 1,000 miles from the Atlantic, and at Iquitos, Peru, 1,300 miles farther upstream.

The floodplain of the Amazon is relatively narrow downstream from Manaus, where it occupies a fault depression between the highlands on either side. To the west, the basin broadens until it abuts the base of the Andes in Colombia, Ecuador, Peru, and Bolivia. It is a plain of gentle gradient and little relief, much of it inundated for months each year. A "fall line" restricts the floodplain on the south to the lower reaches of the tributaries originating in the Central Highlands.

The Central Highlands. The highlands, which constitute the seemingly endless expanses of central Brazil and its extension along the Southern Plateau, are the source of many Amazon tributaries including the Tapajós, the Xingú, the Araguaia, and the Tocantins —names which still conjure up images of unexplored territory, perilous expeditions, and remote savages. The São Francisco, Doce, Paraná, and Paraguay Rivers are also born in the Central Highlands, all except the Paraguay being interrupted not far from their mouths by falls and rapids which mark their descent from the uplands.

Most of this region, except for some peripheral lava flows and sedimentary formations, is a peneplain of ancient rocks uplifted 1,000 to 4,000 feet above sea level. The level to gently rolling surface is here and there interrupted by deep canyons or broken by the stumps of eroded mountains. Most of the latter are only one or two thousand feet higher than the plateau, but the Pico de Itatiaia in the Serra da Mantiqueira attains 9,255 feet elevation. These ranges are the principal mineralized zones in Brazil, the most diversified of which is the Serra do Espinhaço, rising behind Belo Horizonte and extending northward to the banks of the São Francisco River in Bahia.

To the southwest, the Central Highlands end in a sandstone escarpment flanking the nearly featureless lowland known as the Pantanal, or Great Swamp. Five hundred miles long and 100 wide, it includes parts of Bolivia, Paraguay, and Argentina. The natural levees of the Paraguay River and occasional hummocks provide refuge for man and beast during the rainy season, when the land may be flooded to depths of up to twelve feet.

In the east, the Central Highlands terminate along the Atlantic in an abrupt fault escarpment known as the Serra do Mar. Extending from Bahia to Rio Grande do Sul, it averages about 3,000 feet above sea level; but the various ranges in which it culminates along the Rio de Janeiro and Epírito Santo borders have peaks which surpass 9,000 feet. Uncut by navigable rivers, the Serra do Mar has always been a formidable barrier to communications between the Central Highlands and the Coastal Lowlands.

The Coastal Lowlands. In many places the Serra do Mar drops directly into the sea in steep, foam-flecked headlands. Elsewhere it is separated from the shoreline by a belt of sand dunes, lagoons, coastal terraces, and alluvial plains that may, particularly north of Cabo Frio, be up to 100 miles wide. Constricted and broken into discontinuous segments, these coastal lowlands have, despite their isolation from each other, been until very recently the principal foci of Brazilian settlement (Map 4).

Only in the extreme north and south of the country do the coastal plains lead inland. At the delta of the Amazon, they merge into the world's largest equatorial lowland. Along the southern rim of the plateau, known here as the Serra Geral, they blend into the rolling plains of Rio Grande do Sul, a grassland that grades into the temperate Pampas of Uruguay and Argentina. Between these extremes of rain forest and prairie lie the varied climates of Brazil and their related soil and vegetation patterns.

THE CLIMATE

The Brazilian climate does not include the excesses of cold, heat, or drought such as one may find in the United States; but it does exhibit wide variety within the range from sub-humid to humid and from sub-tropical to tropical. Average annual rainfall may vary from less than 20 inches in the Northeast to over 200 inches along the escarpment behind Santos. In the South and in certain mountain areas frosts occur regularly; whereas in the Amazon a cold wave, or *friagem,* is considered to have struck when temperatures drop below 65° Fahrenheit. With allowances for minor, but at times significant, variations within them, Brazil's climates may be characterized by a few major regions (Map 5): the humid tropics, subdivided into equatorial, tropical coast, and tropical interior expressions; the wet-dry tropics; the sub-tropics, differentiated into a highland type, caused by higher elevation, and a lowland type, created by higher latitude; and, finally, the semi-arid climate region.

Characteristic types of vegetation correspond roughly to the main climates (Map 6): "jungle" in the humid tropics; scrub woods in the wet-dry regions; thorn scrub, or *caatinga,* in the semi-arid zone; and pine forests and grasslands in the sub-tropics. Not infrequently, though, specific plant formations will depart from the regional norm in response to minor variations in the milieu, particularly where they involve topography or ground water conditions. Such changes in the general picture include, for instance, extensive grasslands within the Amazonian and Paraguayan jungles; dense "gallery" forests along the streams that traverse the scrub woods of the Central Highlands; and scrub formations along the coastal strip in Rio Grande do Sul.

Soils are closely linked to vegetation, but their fertility is also affected by the type of underlying rock and the age of the parent material from which they derive. Therefore, although relatively poor ferralitic soils predominate over much of Brazil, there are places with naturally fertile soils. Ranging from those on recent alluviums in the Amazon Basin to the *terra roxa* soils derived from the basalts of the Southern Plateau, Brazil's fertile soils add up to a significant area of land available for productive agriculture. Nevertheless, the high temperatures and heavy rains of the tropics are not conducive to the development of highly productive soils without the addition of fertilizers.

The Humid Tropics. The equatorial phase of the humid tropical climate is illustrated by figures from the climate station at Manaus (Table 1), located not far above sea level in the heart of the Amazon Lowland. Here monthly temperature means vary by only 3° throughout the year. Although average temperatures are around 80° for any given 24-hour period, the mercury rarely reaches 100° at midday and the nights are cool, with temperatures in the low 70's. The warmest months coincide with those which are also the driest and therefore the sunniest; whereas "winter" comes with the cooling downpours of the wet season, which lasts from December to March. No month is really dry, although the rainfall at Manaus is somewhat less during July and August than it is at most equatorial stations. As a result, Manaus' 70 inches per year is at the lower end of the precipitation scale for this type of climate. Seventy-five to 80 inches are more common values in the equatorial region, and Belém has a total of 85 inches average annual rainfall.

South of the equatorial region seasonal differences are much more pronounced. The wet-dry tropics of the Central Plateau will be treated separately, but the lowland stations at Rio de Janeiro and Corumbá are representative extensions of the humid tropics. Here the winter months are about 10 F.° cooler than the warm, rainy period of mid-summer, which differs little from that of the Amazon lowlands at the same time of year. Equatorial conditions persist in the Pantanal for about seven months; but because of the moderating effect of the sea, summer is at its peak in Rio de Janeiro for only

TABLE 1

Representative Climate Stations

Type of Climate	Station and elev. in feet		Jan.	Feb.	Mar.	Apr.	May	Jun.	Jul.	Aug.	Sep.	Oct.	Nov.	Dec.	Year
Equatorial	Manaus 148	temp. °F	79.9	80.1	79.7	79.9	80.1	80.1	80.6	81.7	82.8	82.8	82.2	80.6	81.0
		ppt., ins.	9.2	9.0	9.6	8.5	7.0	3.6	2.2	1.4	2.0	4.1	5.5	7.7	69.8
Tropical, Humid Coast	Rio de Janeiro 197	temp. °F	78.6	79.0	77.7	75.2	72.0	69.6	68.7	69.6	70.3	71.8	73.9	76.6	73.6
		ppt., ins.	4.9	4.8	5.2	4.3	3.1	2.3	1.7	1.7	2.6	3.2	4.1	5.4	43.3
Tropical, Humid Interior	Corumbá 381	temp. °F	80.2	79.5	80.1	78.6	73.9	69.4	70.5	72.7	76.6	78.4	79.9	80.1	76.7
		ppt., ins.	6.4	6.7	4.8	5.0	3.3	1.9	0.3	1.3	2.3	3.9	6.0	7.4	49.2
Wet-dry Tropics	Goiás 1,706	temp. °F	74.3	74.8	75.4	75.9	74.7	72.3	72.3	75.2	78.1	77.7	76.1	74.7	75.1
		ppt., ins.	11.9	11.7	11.4	5.0	0.4	0.5	0.0	0.4	1.8	4.8	8.7	10.2	66.8
Wet-dry Tropics	Belo Horizonte 2,812	temp. °F	71.4	72.1	71.1	68.7	65.5	62.6	62.2	64.4	68.4	70.3	70.3	70.2	68.1
		ppt., ins.	12.8	9.5	6.3	2.9	0.6	0.5	0.4	0.9	1.5	4.9	8.3	10.7	59.3
Sub-tropical Highlands	Curitiba 2,979	temp. °F	68.7	70.0	66.7	62.2	56.7	54.0	54.5	56.3	58.3	61.0	64.4	67.3	61.7
		ppt., ins.	6.6	6.3	4.4	3.1	4.0	4.0	2.5	3.2	4.9	5.5	5.0	5.5	55.0
Sub-tropical Lowlands	Porto Alegre 49	temp. °F	76.1	76.5	72.9	68.9	63.0	56.3	56.5	58.3	61.7	65.1	70.2	73.8	66.6
		ppt., ins.	4.3	3.7	3.6	4.8	4.1	5.0	4.3	5.1	4.6	3.1	3.3	4.1	50.0
Semi-arid	Quixeramobim 679	temp. °F	82.9	81.9	80.8	80.4	79.5	79.2	79.5	80.8	82.0	82.9	83.3	83.5	81.4
		ppt., ins.	3.7	4.3	7.0	7.0	5.2	2.5	1.3	0.6	0.1	0.1	0.4	1.4	33.6

Source: P. E. James, *Latin America*.

three or four months of the year. The colder winters are due to polar air from Antarctic source regions flowing northward across the Paraguay lowland and along the Atlantic coast, which outbreaks cause temperatures to drop into the 40's at both Rio and Corumbá. A greater amount of winter rain falls at the former of the two stations because the Atlantic cell of polar air brings with it moisture from the sea, while its western component has traversed only the dry interior of Argentina and Paraguay before reaching Corumbá.

The Wet-dry Tropics. The climate figures for the town of Goiás, on the Central Plateau not far from Brasília but at somewhat lower elevation, reflect the distinctive feature that gives the wet-dry tropics their name: the extreme seasonality of the precipitation regime. During the six-month dry season, from mid-April to mid-October, a high pressure system on the plateau becomes a source of outflowing cool, dry air. At this time the region takes on the characteristics of a desert, with one-half inch of rain or less falling during four of these months; in fact, July has never recorded any precipitation. On the other hand, the four months at the height of the rainy season have values that exceed those in the equatorial region. At this time heating in the interior of the continent creates a monsoon effect, drawing humid air in from both the North and South Atlantic.

Elevations ranging from 1,500 to 4,500 feet give the Central Plateau an exceptionally pleasant climate. Thus Goiás' 1,700 foot elevation reduces sea level temperatures by approximately 6 F.°; whereas corrected temperatures would be similar to those at Manaus.

Six hundred miles to the southeast, Belo Horizonte exhibits wider seasonal temperature differences than Goiás because of its greater distance from the equator. The range is of about the same order of magnitude as at Rio de Janeiro, but the diminution of temperature with elevation at Belo Horizonte is less pronounced because the moderating effect of the sea tends to reduce temperatures at the coastal station. As Belo Horizonte is more distant from equatorial moisture source regions, the rainy season is shorter there than it is at Goiás; on the other hand, more rain falls there during the dry season because of cyclonic storms which accompany the occasional flow of polar air masses onto the margins of the Central Plateau.

The Sub-tropics. Curitiba, at about the same elevation as Belo Horizonte but 500 miles farther south, has a markedly cooler climate, particularly in winter. This places it in the sub-tropics, rather than the tropics, the boundary between which coincides roughly with the southern limit of coffee growing and the northern border of the *Araucaria,* or Paraná Pine forests. Although the fact is not evident from the mean monthly figures of Table 1, the regular occurrence of frost at Curitiba in winter is associated with the outbreak of polar air which brings below-freezing temperatures to the Southern Plateau and the Rio Grande do Sul Plains. These air masses are accompanied by the passage of cold fronts which produce, at both Curitiba and Porto Alegre, mean monthly precipitation values of 2.5 to 5.5 inches in winter and spring—higher than those at any of the other Brazilian stations shown at this time of year.

Differences between the figures for Curitiba, on the plateau, and Porto Alegre, on the plains, are a function of elevation and latitude. Mean monthly temperatures are consistently lower at Curitiba, despite its more northerly location, because of its situation at 3,000 feet above sea level. On the other hand, higher latitude accounts for the greater seasonal range of temperature at Porto Alegre. While the latter's position closer to the source regions of polar air and its associated cyclonic storms brings that station more winter precipitation, it receives less summer rainfall than does Curitiba as it is farther from the equatorial moisture sources. Porto Alegre's longer, hotter summers reflect the fact that temperatures there are not reduced by elevation, being only slightly lower than those at Rio de Janeiro, in the tropics 1,000 miles to the north.

The Semi-arid Region. The highest average and absolute temperatures in Brazil are recorded in the semi-arid heartland of the Northeast. This is the only part of Brazil which is not classified as humid. The 34 inches average annual rainfall at Quixeramobim, in the interior of Ceará, seems at first glance to be an amount that is at least adequate for farming, even though it is appreciably less than elsewhere in the country. In "normal" years this is, just barely, the case; but other stations have lower values, and clear skies and high temperatures increase the rate of evaporation and reduce the effectiveness of what precipitation there is. In fact, evaporation exceeds precipitation throughout the region. As a consequence, the natural vegetation consists of desert plants and thorn scrub known as *caatinga,* an Indian word meaning "white woods." The only permanent stream which crosses this area is the São Francisco, which like the Nile, or the Colorado in North America, gets its water from rains that fall on remote mountain slopes, in this case in Minas Gerais and southern Bahia.

The principal problem of the Northeast is, however, not so much a mean shortage of precipitation as its extreme and unpredictable irregularity from one year to the next. Long term studies have shown that about half the years over the past century have had "abnormal" rainfall conditions; whereas nowhere else in the country did the figure exceed 20 percent. This phenomenon is caused by fluctuations in the position of the Intertropical Front, which brings the summer rains to those areas beyond the equatorial region. Excessively high pressures over the South Atlantic keep the Intertropical Front from penetrating much beyond the western margins of the Northeast. Conversely, abnormally low pressures over that ocean cause the front to remain over the area for unusually long periods, also increasing the intensity of its tropical convergence storms. For this reason, there are times when no rain falls at all for twelve months or more; or there may be weeks of heavy rainfall that being widespread flooding. Months of drought are often followed by calamitous downpours, and "normal" years corresponding to the averages are the exception rather than the rule. This inhospitable environment supports only a sparse population which during periods of drought or flood pours, possessionless and hungry, into the coastal cities or other, more humid regions of Brazil.

REGIONALISM AND HISTORY

Although it would be an oversimplification to state that the cultural and economic variety of Brazil's regions derives from their physical environments, there can be little doubt that the divers landforms, climates, vegetation complexes, and soils have played an important role in differentiating the evolutionary paths of various parts of the country.

In the early days of colonization it was the easily accessible tropical coast, with its suitability for producing crops complementary to those of Europe, which brought to that area colonial Brazil's greatest development, income, and population densities. Before the evolution of the coast was complete, bands of independent backwoodsmen roamed the vast scrub-covered uplands in search of slaves, gold, and diamonds, leaving their legacy to the hardy cattle-raising society that has persisted to the present day throughout much of the interior.

Later on, during the Empire, the humid highland climates behind the Serra do Mar provided the ideal environment for coffee growing, which definitively shifted the focus of Brazilian prosperity to the East. Emancipation of the slaves attracted tides of settlers from Europe to the more southerly states, where both tropical crops and those of their homeland could be grown side by side. The knowledge and energy of these immigrants combined with the toughness and native ability of the descendants of the pioneers to give São Paulo and the South a standard of living, based on both agriculture and industry, in every way comparable to that of large parts of Europe. By contrast, in the Amazon, a large proportion of its few inhabitants continue to live under conditions which have scarcely changed since the day the first Europeans set foot on what is now Brazilian soil.

2 *Evolution of a Brazilian Civilization*

Every nation is the product of its people and of the environment in which they live. Because of complex interrelationships between man and the land during the course of history, each nation differs from every other. But many countries resemble, to some degree, neighboring or more distant ones with similar environments, peoples, or cultures. A few are unique—truly unlike any found elsewhere on the globe. Brazil is such a nation.

Claimed by its inhabitants to be the only European civilization in the tropics, Brazil has nevertheless blended Amerindian and African qualities into the basic Portuguese culture, itself an amalgam of Celtic, Roman, Hispanic, Germanic, and North African traits. Peoples and influences from Europe and the Middle East, from other parts of the Americas, and from as far away as Japan have gradually been added, to produce a culture which is neither European nor "tropical," but distinctively and exuberantly Brazilian.

Within the general unity and cohesiveness of Brazilian culture, there are subcultures which are primarily regional in origin and expression, although racial and social criteria have also played a part in their differentiation. In their extremes, these subcultures range from those of modern urbanism in the East and South to Indian tribal patterns at various stages of "Brazilianization" in the North and West. Still, there is cultural harmony throughout, which is, in part, an outgrowth of the openness of the Luso-Brazilian temperament, with its uncritical acceptance of the differences in people, their ideas, and their way of life.

18

This forebearance is applied not only to those within the Luso-Brazilian culture group, but equally to any strangers with whom they may come in contact. This last statement is also applicable, at least to some degree, to relations with the Amerindians from whom the land was gradually wrested. That is not to say that Brazilian history lacked those black pages of enslavement and slaughter that characterized European occupation of the New World; but in Brazil the excesses were often tempered by a certain humanity and even respect, which were sadly lacking in most other colonial areas.[1]

THE INDIANS

Numerically there are now few pure Indians left in Brazil: perhaps 100,000 in contrast to the one million that were estimated to have been in the area before the Europeans arrived. Indians constitute only .15 percent of the Brazilian population, compared to .3 percent among the larger United States total; but there is far more Indian blood in the general racial composition of the former. Furthermore, many among Brazil's so-called Indians are scarcely distinguishable physically and culturally from the surrounding "Brazilians." Conversely, through association and intermarriage during the early days of colonial settlement, the Indian influence on the present Brazilian culture has been of lasting, if at times subtle significance.

The ancestors of these indigenous Brazilians were probably among the earliest of the many waves of people of Mongoloid stock who wandered into the Americas from Asia. Archaeological finds place them in cave dwellings in the present state of Minas Gerais some 10,000 years ago and on the *sambaquís,* or kitchen middens, of the São Paulo and Paraná coast at least 8,000 years ago. Most of the

[1] Early in 1968 Brazilians were shocked by a report that Indians were being exploited by whites in remote areas. Even worse, officials at outposts of the Indian Protection Service had condoned, or were involved in land seizures, murder, and the enslavement of young girls for domestic service. As a result, the Service, which had won worldwide renown for the self-sacrifice of its unarmed personnel in making peaceful contact with the natives, was closed down and 134 of its officials face criminal charges.

Amerindians of Brazil belonged to a linguistic group known as Tupí-Guaraní, which included as wide a variety of languages as the Indo-European family. Lesser groups were also found within the present national borders, including the Caribs and Arawaks, who ranged from the Amazon Basin to the islands of the Caribbean.

Differing sharply from the tribes of the principal Spanish settlements, especially in Mexico and Peru, the Brazilian Indian presented no high order of civilization, accomplishment, or accumulated wealth for the plunder of the European arrivals. There were among them some groups which are presumed to have been more advanced than others, although the differences cannot have been very great. For instance, at Santarém and on Marajó Island elaborate ceramics have been unearthed; and it is known that by the main stream of the Amazon and continuing along the coast as far south as the island on which São Luís is now located, there were fairly large permanent settlements of 500 to 1,500 inhabitants. But for the most part villages were small and dispersed, with tribal units fragmented into clans of only a few dozen households.

Under the system based on shifting land occupancy which generally prevailed, no pressure could be brought to bear by chiefs or shamans to induce the members of their tribe to perform the prodigious labors which were required to build such civilizations as those of the Aztecs, the Mayas, or the Incas, for whom escape across hostile deserts, mountains, and jungles was impossible. In the Brazilian environment it was a simple matter, if some chieftain became too overbearing or demanding, to put one's belongings into a canoe and paddle downstream to a new and virgin patch of forest every bit as good as the land from which one had come. There a new hut or settlement, perhaps even a tribe, could be set up.

It was into this unstable human environment of virtually uninhibited freedom that the European first intruded. And it was here that the Indian succeeded in inculcating in the traditionally land-frugal Portuguese the practice of slash-and-burn agriculture. This shifting occupancy of such a seemingly endless territory—and of all the nations in the world Brazil has perhaps the greatest expanse of verdant nature—undoubtedly contributed to the subsequent Brazilian concept of land as an expendable resource, to be used briefly and then abandoned for greener fields. More prosaically, the Indian was also responsible for the adoption of the hammock to replace the bed throughout the North and Northeast of Brazil; and many Indian words have enriched the Brazilian version of the Portuguese language, particularly those for a wide range of foodstuffs, both indigenous and European.

Space does not permit fuller treatment of the various Indian groups in Brazil, many of which have long since vanished from the scene. Suffice it to say that the differences between them were often of life and death significance to the Europeans who established themselves on these shores. There were, for instance, the peaceful Goianás of the Tietê River in present-day São Paulo, who migrated between the highlands in summer and the warm coast in wintertime. They welcomed the newcomers and guided them along the trails they had established so that effective inland settlement and expansion was easily achieved during the first few decades of the European presence within their realm. On the other hand, a tribe of warlike Tupí Indians disrupted communications and prevented settlement of the Rio Doce valley until 1910! In many of the streams tributary to the Amazon there are still tribes living much as they did before the Europeans arrived, who will shoot on sight any strangers entering their territory.

DISCOVERY AND EARLY SETTLEMENT

The discovery of Brazil has traditionally been assigned to the Portuguese navigator Pedro Alvarez Cabral, in 1500.[2] Whatever the merits of the case, it is recorded that in 1502, 105 years before the first North American colonists landed at Jamestown, trading posts were established at Salvador in Bahia and at Cabo Frio in the present state of Rio de Janeiro. Others followed, including some

[2] For an alternative possibility, see Chapter 6. The question of Brazil's discovery is discussed, in interesting detail, in Edgar Prestage, *The Portuguese Pioneers,* Adam and Charles Black, London, 1966, Chapter 11.

that were French. Most were little more than a single hut occupied
by a trader, who exchanged European manufactures for Brazilwood
supplied by the Indians. Cut from the forests of the coastal lowlands
it was shipped to Europe for making a much-prized red dye. This
dense tree, which gave the country its name, was a reddish color
like burning coals, or *brazas*.

In 1530 the Portuguese Crown decided to regularize and stimulate
the haphazard settlement along the Brazilian coast, especially to
guard against mounting encroachments by the French and Spanish.
For this purpose the coast was divided into *Capitanías,* which were
extended an indefinite distance into the unexplored wilderness, or
sertão. Each was run by a Captain-General sent out by the Crown.
He was supposed to establish a colonial nucleus in his area, but
compliance depended largely upon the conscientiousness of the individual.

The first of the settlements under the Capitanía system was at
São Vicente, in 1532, the same year in which a renegade Portuguese
sailor became the first European to reach the wilderness beyond the
coastal escarpment. Marrying into an Indian tribe, he settled near
the present city of São Paulo, the cordiality of his reception soon attracting other whites to the tribal villages. The second official Portuguese colony was established at Olinda, near present-day Recife, in
1537.

Not until 1555 was a colony founded in the magnificent Guanabara Bay, where Rio de Janeiro is now situated. This was a French
settlement at a fort which had been built on one of the bay's many
islands to harass the Portuguese in the area. Ten years later the
Portuguese built a fort of their own at the mouth of the bay, at
the foot of Sugar Loaf Mountain. From this base they drove out
the French and their Indian allies in a naval battle in 1567.

Early colonization of Brazil was, at best, halting and sporadic,
as it continued to be in subsequent periods of development and of
opening up the country's interior. In any case, in the context of
those early exciting days of the European Age of Discovery, the
colony suffered from a certain lack of appeal. For one thing, the

ndian inhabitants offered no particularly attractive source of plunder, either human or material. For another, during the first century after its discovery, there was no apparent source of ready wealth in Brazil to direct Portugal's attention away from the lucrative trade routes to Africa and Asia. Lastly, the 3,000-foot escarpment just back of the coast presented a formidable obstacle to penetration of the center and south, while the Northeast was backed by semi-desert, and the North provided only a hostile and impenetrable, Indian-infested jungle. Only the narrow coastal plain offered a modicum of accessible space on which to establish a foothold, but it had little to offer for export except Brazilwood and a few minor tropical products. Such was the situation until the colonists were strong enough and knowledgeable enough to develop their own exotic source of revenue: sugar.

SUGAR CANE: FIRST OF THE BOOMS

From 1530 when the Capitanía system was established, the Crown also began parcelling out tracts of land, known as *sesmarias,* to private individuals. Some of these were enormous: a single grant, for instance, included all of what is now the state of Sergipe. Others were of more modest dimensions, such as those around the bay at Salvador, where the soil was found to be superior for tobacco growing. It was to work on the tobacco plantations of this area, known as the *Recôncavo,* that the first African slaves were brought to Brazil in 1538.

Elsewhere in Brazil there was neither the need for slave labor nor the money to purchase slaves until, in the 1560's, sugar cane began to be grown in ever increasing quantities to meet a rising demand for that product in Europe. The cultivation of sugar had spread northward from the São Vicente-Santos region, where the first plantings had been introduced from Madeira Island in the 1530's, to the lowlands around Rio de Janeiro, Salvador, and Recife. African slaves were brought into Pernambuco in 1567 to work on the sugar plantations, and this area became the center from which the practice of systematic cane planting by slave labor spread to

other parts of the Northeast. In the region between Guanabara Bay
and Campos, at the mouth of the Paraíba River, the earlier practice
of using Indian labor on the sugar plantations persisted until about
1590. The natives were less effective workers than the Africans,
however, and Rio de Janeiro subsequently became one of the
principal importers of slaves in the colony.

Although the cultivation of sugar began at São Vicente, production there lagged because the cost of shipping the product to Europe
from this, the most southerly outpost of Portuguese colonization,
was very high and because the settlers were too poor to import
slaves. They had to rely on a dwindling supply of Indian labor sold
to them by the São Paulo *Bandeirantes*. The latter were migratory
bands of explorers who, with their Indian allies, for two centuries
ranged the interior from the headwaters of the Amazon to the
estuary of the La Plata in search of gold and slaves.

During the last part of the sixteenth century and for most of
the seventeenth, Brazil, especially the Northeast, was Europe's
major supplier of sugar. However, a high proportion of the financing, marketing, and refining was in the hands of the Dutch, who
eventually decided they should obtain control over the entire productive process. This they attempted to do in 1624 by capturing
Salvador from the Portuguese and São Luís do Maranhão from the
French, who had founded a colony there in 1612. They were soon
driven out of their foothold in Bahia, but merely shifted their attention northward and captured Recife. The Portuguese homeland
was too busy with its affairs in other parts of the world to take
effective measures against this encroachment, and the Dutch hegemony was extended over that part of the Brazilian coast which lay
between the mouth of the Amazon and northern Bahia. The Portuguese colonists then, on their own initiative, organized an army
which gradually drove out the Dutch, placing São Luís under the
Portuguese flag in 1644 and forcing the Dutch to abandon Recife
ten years later.

The long-range effect of this action against the Dutch was to awaken a Brazilian national consciousness. But it had the immediate adverse effect of sending the Dutch elsewhere with the knowledge of techniques of sugar production which they had acquired in Brazil. They established plantations in Barbados, whence this activity spread to other parts of the Caribbean. By the end of the seventeenth century the more modern and efficient West Indian plantations were capturing the European sugar market from Brazil, where productivity had already begun to decline because plantation owners failed to make the necessary investments to modernize and remain in a competitive position.

Although Brazil thenceforward lost all significance in the world sugar market, the period of the sugar boom was fundamental to the development of many of the nation's socio-economic institutions. Attitudes formed by a landowning sugar plantation aristocracy dominated the thinking of the Brazilian upper-class everywhere until very recently, and still predominate in certain parts of the country. Land ownership is believed to confer privileges and prerogatives upon the landowner, who feels very little obligation toward the land or those who work it. The corollary to this is the belief in the inherently inferior position of the servile masses, a concept brought originally from Portugal and reinforced by the introduction of slavery.

These anachronistic socio-economic views continue to influence the thinking of a majority of the "old families" throughout Brazil, particularly those living in the cattle lands of the interior and in the coastal regions from Rio de Janeiro to the Amazon. They consider that the human and natural resources of the country exist solely for their own personal benefit. In practice, this outlook may be reflected in rural areas by denudation of the soil, with little thought given to its long-term productivity, and even less to the illiterate and impoverished peasants who work it. In the cities, this attitude has led to the deriving of unconscionable profits from the toil and misery of the *favelados,* or shantytown dwellers. The gold mining period which followed the sugar cycle only served to reinforce this exploitative attitude that originated with slash-and-burn farming and the subjugation of the Indian and became institutionalized under the sugar plantation and slavery.

THE GOLD CYCLE

In 1694 the *Bandeirantes'* century and a half search for precious metals in the interior was finally rewarded by the discovery of gold in the mountains of what was then the northeastern part of São Paulo Province, a vast territory that extended the nearly anarchic hegemony of the São Paulo *Bandeirantes* over all of central and southern Brazil. Twenty years later diamonds were found in the same area.

As these events came at the time of a crucial decline in income from sugar, many plantation owners moved with their slaves from the coast into the mining area to exploit this new resource. In a series of small battles, Northeasterners drove out the vastly outnumbered *Paulistas* to gain control over the surrounding region. This invasion brought about the establishment of the separate province of Minas Gerais ("General Mines") in 1720. In 1748, after gold was discovered in the West, Goiás and Mato Grosso were also separated from São Paulo. Official attention was now directed toward what had been a land of little consequence to the sugar-oriented coastal populace until gold gave it value.

Motivated primarily by a desire to control the taxes levied on gold production, colonial authorities for the first time asserted firm rule over the Brazilian backlands. This move accompanied the building of a road from Rio de Janeiro to the mining area in 1705, thus at long last connecting that city directly to the lands beyond the Serra do Mar. Other routes followed, and settlements and towns arose at the mine fields and also, although very sparsely, on the lands between. Income from the mines shifted the focus of Brazilian economic and political activity from the sugar fields of the northeastern coast to the central part of the country. This trend culminated in the transfer of the Vice-Regal capital from Salvador to Rio de Janeiro in 1763. By 1800 the latter city had a population of

100,000. Salvador and Recife each had 70,000 inhabitants. São Paulo, Ouro Preto (the principal mining center and capital of Minas Gerais), and São Luís lagged well behind, with populations of about 20,000 apiece. Santos, with 7,000 inhabitants, was the only other city in Brazil with a population over 5,000.

NEW CENTER OF THE PORTUGUESE EMPIRE

Income from the mines started to decline in the 1780's, and the boom was definitely over by the turn of the century. But the momentum and wealth which it had engendered, and the lack of new sources of national income, ensured the continued dominance of Rio de Janeiro in the country's affairs. Then, in 1808, Dom João VI of Portugal moved his court to that city after the homeland was occupied by Napoleon.

For all practical purposes, the arrival of the Court in Rio marked the end of Brazil's colonial status, as it now became the administrative seat of the Portuguese Empire. Royal interest in this, by far the largest of all of Portugal's possessions, was paramount and direct. Official energies were directed toward trying to unify and develop this sprawling land, albeit in piecemeal and often ineffective fashion. Central authority was consolidated; Brazilian income remained within the country instead of being siphoned off to Portugal; roads were improved, at least in the area immediately adjoining Rio de Janeiro; and small contingents of colonists from Europe were settled in the cool highlands of the Serra do Mar and on the temperate plains of Rio Grande do Sul, where they were supposed to fill the demographic vacuum between the Portuguese realm and the Spanish colonies to the south.

In 1821 Dom João returned to Portugal, leaving his son Pedro behind to rule the virtually autonomous Brazilian colony. In the following year Pedro declared Brazil an independent empire, and assumed the title of Emperor Dom Pedro I. In 1831 his five-year-old son succeeded to the throne, and for the next ten years the country was under a regency. The new Emperor, Pedro II, was to reign for 55 years, during which he gained fame for his successful economic, diplomatic, and cultural policies. He became recognized as one of the most intelligent and enlightened monarchs of his time.

Brazil's peaceful change from colonial to independent status and its preservation under a single flag of all the Portuguese territory in South America, were in strong contrast to the bitter fighting in and the fragmentation of the Spanish colonies in the New World. One reason, certainly, was that the Luso-Brazilian rulers were rational and moderate; another was that Portugal had exercised less rigid and autocratic authority over its colonies than had Spain; and, finally, stability and prosperity were provided by the next boom product, coffee.

THE COFFEE BOOM

Coffee was first grown for home consumption on the hillsides around the city of Rio de Janeiro in 1760. From here it spread along the routes to the mines, into the highlands beyond the Serra do Mar, where production centered on the drainage basin of the Paraíba River. The first modest shipment of coffee was exported in 1779, and it became a regular item of trade from 1813 onward. Production increased rapidly: to 10,000 tons in 1820 and 30,000 a decade later.

During the first half of the nineteenth century, nine-tenths of Brazil's coffee came from the interior of Rio de Janeiro Province, where many small towns and fine plantations arose, linked to the capital by a gradually improving network of roads. Much of the income from coffee remained in Rio, where the landed aristocracy, or "coffee barons," lived at least part of the year and formed the nucleus of the Imperial Court. As coffee exports brought about a general economic expansion, some of the wealthier and more imaginative of the coffee nobility organized industrial, banking, and transport enterprises, especially railroads, laying the foundation for an incipient capitalism.

In 1852 Brazil's first railroad was built, from the head of

Guanabara Bay to the base of the Serra do Mar, to transport both coffee and the wealthy *Cariocas,* who, with the Royal Family, summered in the mountain resort of Petrópolis. Twelve more years were to pass, however, before the first railroad surmounted the formidable escarpment behind Rio to serve the main coffee producing area in the middle Paraíba Valley. Two years after that, in 1866, a second set of rails crossed the escarpment, joining Santos to São Paulo. In both regions, once the coastal barrier had been overcome and outlets provided to the two principal seaports at Rio and Santos, railroads spread across the highlands beyond. But whereas the railroads of Rio Province and southern Minas Gerais followed the old coffee roads and simply provided a new means for exporting the produce of an established agricultural zone, those in São Paulo to a large extent penetrated into sparsely used lands, opening up new areas to coffee. Therefore, while from the 1850's to the 1880's coffee production in Rio de Janeiro remained stable at about 100,000 tons a year, that of São Paulo was steadily overtaking it. Production in Minas Gerais also increased, although at a slower rate than in São Paulo, as more distant agricultural areas began to be served by this new means of transport.

During the third quarter of the nineteenth century Brazil enjoyed the peak prosperity of one more of its boom cycles. Then, in 1888, the slaves were emancipated by decree of Dom Pedro's daughter, Isabel, while she was acting as Regent during one of the Emperor's numerous trips abroad. With the sudden loss of their slaves, representing most of their invested capital and virtually all of their labor force, the planters abandoned the plantations of Rio de Janeiro, and the baronial coffee economy collapsed. With it went the Empire. The conservative plantation owners allied themselves with the liberal anti-monarchists and the military, who disliked the idea of having to deal with Isabel and her unpopular husband upon the death of the Emperor, and forced Dom Pedro II to abdicate and leave the country in exile. Brazil was proclaimed a Republic on November 15, 1889.

EARLY YEARS OF THE REPUBLIC

Rio de Janeiro, still the main entrepôt and commercial city of Brazil, remained the center of the new republican government. At this time, national politics were carried out on the basis of balances struck among the oligarchies that controlled each of the states' political apparatus. These oligarchies were made up of or controlled by the *coronéis,* the large landowners who commanded all social and economic as well as political power in their districts. The system was at first dominated by the *coronéis* from the Northeast and Rio de Janeiro, in much the same way as the plantation aristocracy from the Southeast dominated politics in the early years of the United States of America. However, with the disintegration of the economic base in the former slave plantation areas, power gradually shifted to those two large and productive states of the Brazilian East, São Paulo and Minas Gerais.

Both São Paulo and Minas Gerais had overtaken Rio de Janeiro State in coffee production by 1890. While Minas went on to build a stable economy based on mineral exports and a varied agricultural production, São Paulo continued to concentrate on coffee. The latter state soon became the world's largest producer of that commodity in a rapidly expanding market. These two political units were to assume ever greater importance in the economic and political structure of the country as the years went by.

Not only did the geographic center of coffee production shift dramatically during the last decade of the nineteenth century, but the structure of the industry changed completely. From the slavery of the Empire it evolved into an entrepreneurial system based on free, if tenant, labor, much of which was provided by immigrants. They were especially attracted to São Paulo, which state received 3 million of the 4.6 million newcomers who settled in Brazil between 1890 and 1930. The new tenant, in contrast to his lackadaisical and unmotivated predecessor, the slave, was a highly productive individual. He hoped to save enough money some day to buy land of his own. He wanted to provide himself with a standard of living at least as high as that which he had enjoyed in the country he had left behind. And, unlike the subservient tenant on the old semi-feudal plantation, he insisted on exercising the political freedom he expected to enjoy when he came to the New World.

The São Paulo plantation owner—unlike his aristocratic predecessor who disdained the mundane routine of business as long as his overseer provided him with an income suited to his usual standard of living—was actively interested in the agricultural and financial affairs of his estate. Furthermore, the new tenant system freed capital that would previously have been needed to purchase slaves, for other forms of investment. In São Paulo especially, funds made available from the profits of coffee growing were invested in agricultural improvements, better communications, and manufacturing plants. From the last came more and more of the products needed to satisfy the demands for higher living standards by the people of that state particularly, but by those in other parts of the country as well.

Apart from fundamental changes in the coffee industry, there was a general shift in Brazil's economic orientation. At the end of the Empire there were only 626 industrial establishments in the country; whereas between 1890 and 1914 6,946 new plants were built. The process was accelerated during World War I in response to a shortage of imported manufactured goods. As industrialization proceeded, so did urbanization. But before these processes were complete, the Great Depression, a long period of dictatorship, and World War II had yet to intervene.

THE "NEW STATE" OF GETÚLIO VARGAS

The Brazilian economy was dealt a severe blow by the 1929 depression, which brought with it political unrest such as was felt in many parts of the world during those unsettled times. In Brazil matters were brought to a head when the 1930 elections were won by the presidential candidate from São Paulo. This challenged the political *status quo* on three counts: the nomination of a candidate not agreed upon by the *coronéis;* his election over the representative of the oligarchy by popular vote of an emergent middle class and a new proletariat of industrial workers; and the repudiation thereby of an understanding between Minas Gerais and São Paulo, endorsed by those in control of the political machinery in the other states, under which their respective candidates were to alternate holding the presidency. This time, it had been the turn of the mining state's nominee.

Armed forces from Minas Gerais, Paraíba, and Rio Grande do Sul now sparked a nationwide revolt, although fighting was limited because of the rapid seizure of Rio de Janeiro and São Paulo by the troops. A military junta took over and Getúlio Vargas, former Governor of Rio Grande do Sul and a large landowner in that state, was named Provisional President in October, 1930. The constitution was dissolved, and the states were placed under the control of Vargas-appointed "interventors." Ironically, although the purpose of the revolution was to reassert the dominance of the *coronéis,* the Vargas dictatorship ultimately proved to be the hot-house in which began to bud the political power of a new urban society—power which reached full flower in 1950.

Under pressure from the coffee planters, Vargas instituted government supports for their crop, the price of coffee having dropped from 4 *mil réis* per kilogram to less than 1 *mil réis* in 1929–30.[3] Between 1931 and 1939 about one-third of the crop was destroyed. But the uneconomic nature of this program is evident from the fact that, with an assured market and price for their product, the coffee growers expanded their production throughout those years

[3] At this time the currency was based on the *real,* a thousand being 1 *mil réis,* written 1$000. Subsequently the monetary unit was changed to the *cruzeiro,* made up of 100 *centavos* each worth 10 *réis,* written Cr$1,00. Inflation has long since rendered both the *real* and the *centavo* meaningless, while the *cruzeiro* had so declined in value since its introduction that on February 8, 1967, President Castelo Branco ordered a currency devaluation and the introduction of a "new cruzeiro" that is worth 1,000 of the old units, or 1 million of the long extinct *réis.* In subsequent sections of this text, values will be expressed in "old" *cruzeiros* since, as in France, it will no doubt be many years before the new monetary terminology gains popular acceptance in Brazil.

at the same rate as coffee was being destroyed. Even worse, not only did government supports subsidize a privileged sector of society, but the artificially high prices and export restrictions in Brazil encouraged the expansion of coffee growing in other countries, notably Colombia, thereby ending Brazil's near-monopolistic position in the world market.

While Vargas was assuring himself of the backing of the powerful plantation owners, particularly in São Paulo and Minas Gerais, he was at the same time building up a personal following among the working classes by passing social measures, providing makework projects, and allowing labor to organize, albeit under strict government supervision. Through political acumen and great personal magnetism, Vargas was able in a few years to gain support from both the upper and lower classes. His power was secured in 1933 when elections, using the secret ballot for the first time in Brazilian history, were held for a Constituent Assembly. A majority of the delegates elected were Vargas supporters, and, after drafting a new constitution, they elected him President for a four year term.

The new constitution was notable in two respects. It dealt in some detail with social matters such as women's suffrage, child labor laws, and minimum wages. And it established the basis for nationalistic sentiments, especially by instituting federal control over the exploitation of natural resources and by restricting the rights of foreigners and foreign corporations in such fields as mining, land ownership, and the professions. To ensure the application of these new measures, the power of the central government was expanded, as was a burgeoning bureaucracy. Brazil started to move away from its previous system with regional diffusion of political power to one of greater federal influence and control.

The dominance of the executive branch of the government in Brazilian politics was assured when, in November 1937, Vargas dissolved Congress and proclaimed himself President for another six years. Replacing the 1934 Constitution with a new one, he assumed the right to make laws by executive decree and to appoint interventors to govern the individual states. This innovation he labeled the "Estado Novo," or New State.

Vargas was now strong enough to permit coffee prices to drop sufficiently to place Brazil back in a competitive position on the world market. But the country could not regain its former monopoly, and World War II soon shrank the overall volume of coffee sales. By 1940 coffee constituted only about one-third of the total value of Brazil's exports. Much of the slack was, however, taken up by greatly increased sales of strategic raw materials; and not long after Pearl Harbor Brazil joined the war on the side of the Allies. She contributed aeroplanes and naval vessels to Atlantic anti-submarine patrols, and sent a six-division expeditionary force to Italy, the only Latin American country to have troops overseas during the conflict.

The war accelerated Brazil's industrial growth, which in turn triggered a general rise in the standard of living, speeded up the process of urbanization, and further increased the political strength of the East. In 1943, as a device to ensure his continued popular support among the growing urban proletariat, Vargas promulgated a labor law which provided benefits for the workers out of all proportion to their productivity and bargaining strength. At the same time he created the Brazilian Labor Party (*Partido Trabalhista Brasileiro* or P.T.B.) as the political arm for organizing this support. The other major parties (since banned) appeared more or less contemporaneously, having been set up either to represent the factions that opposed Vargas or as a façade for power-seeking individuals. These origins have been reflected in their fragmented ideological stands and their dominance by strong political personalities such as former Presidents Kubitschek and Goulart or Presidential hopefuls like Carlos Lacerda of Rio and Adhemar de Barros of São Paulo, all onetime Governors of their respective states.

Despite these new political organizations, apparent harbingers of a return to democratic government, Vargas refused to hold the national elections which were scheduled for shortly after the end of World War II. By this time some of his magic had gone; his proliferating bureaucracy was less and less able to act decisively and effectively; and the economy was ready for more freedom as the country went on a spending spree with the surplus funds accumulated during the war. The man who had led his country out of the depression and through the hostilities was ousted in a bloodless military coup in 1945. His elected successor, Marshal Dutra, was a colorless front man for the military, whose principal claim to fame during five years in office was that he closed down the gambling casinos, unfortunately thereby losing the government a small but steady source of revenue.

Elections were held again in 1950, with Vargas among the presidential candidates. Thanks largely to the popular appeal he still had among the working classes, he was returned to his old office. But the times had changed—or perhaps time had changed the man. Vargas now became more of a demagogue as President than he had been as dictator. While fanning the flames of ultra-nationalism and lower class unrest, he appeared to look the other way as scandals, corruption, and the strong-arm tactics of his entourage outraged and united the various factions that opposed him. This opposition crystallized when an Army officer was shot down while walking home with Carlos Lacerda, then editor of the newspaper which had mounted the most vitriolic of the attacks against Vargas. A delegation from the military demanded Vargas' resignation; instead, on August 24, 1954, he committed suicide.

Thus did Vargas end eighteen years as chief executive, spanning a quarter of a century (1930–1954), or one-third the total life-span of the Republic. Even after his death Vargas' influence was not over, as he left a suicide note which damned foreign imperialism and the forces of evil on the Right, blaming them for Brazil's plight and his own persecution. This legacy became a manifesto to which politicians who claim to be the successors of Vargas still refer, perpetuating the name and the legend. The difficult period through which he steered Brazil and the growth and fundamental changes over which he presided are often forgotten amidst the bitterness over this frequently distorted heritage which his name conjures up today.

NEW STIRRINGS IN BRAZIL

The remainder of Vargas' term was filled competently, if unspectacularly, by his Vice-President, Café Filho, who did not trouble to move into the presidential palace but instead chose to remain in his modest apartment on Copacabana Beach. In 1955 Juscelino Kubitschek, who had been Governor of Minas Gerais, was elected President. But he was not assured of assuming office (in 1956) until the Army announced it would see that he did, thereby putting an end to conservative expectations of possibly blocking his accession. Kubitschek belonged to the Social Democratic Party (P.S.D.) and his Vice-President, João Goulart, former Governor of Rio Grande do Sul and a neighbor of the martyred dictator, belonged to the P.T.B. Each man claimed to be the true heir of Getúlio Vargas.

Kubitschek's five years in office were characterized by a single-minded drive to draw the country together: physically, by improving the woefully inadequate overland transport system; and spiritually, by building a new national capital, Brasília, in the distant interior. He brought the inefficient, hodge-podge railroad system under one central federal authority; forced the establishment of a national automobile industry by punitive duties on imported vehicles; and greatly improved existing arterial roads as well as building new ones, including the spectacular Belém-Brasília Highway, which sliced straight through the Amazon jungle. The climax of Kubitschek's term came in 1960 with the inauguration of Brasília, a city planner's dream high on the Central Plateau. But he failed to curtail the bureaucracy inherited from the days of Vargas, and his vast public works program was financed at the price of a spiraling inflation. History will probably view Kubitschek's presidency as one of imagination and progress; but he left the country in political turmoil, with the forces of Left and Right more sharply defined than at any previous stage in Brazilian history.

Kubitschek's successor was the mercurial Jánio Quadros, former Governor of São Paulo. While holding the latter office, he had compiled a distinguished record of progress and of cleaning out the bureaucracy. The symbol of his campaign was a broom, and it was hoped that he would accomplish the same feats on a national scale. However, he soon found himself at loggerheads with an entrenched conservative Congress and balked by a bureaucratic establishment with which he was unable to come to grips. The one-man rule which had worked so successfully in his home state was simply inappropriate to the lethargic democracy which constituted Brazil's federal power structure. After less than a year in office, Quadros dramatically resigned, blaming his troubles on the selfishness of the Right, their obstruction of his program, and their personal persecution of himself, as epitomized by the attacks of that perpetually dissatisfied oppositionist, Carlos Lacerda. Some political analysts claim that Quadros was hoping to be returned by popular demand and given more power; but if this was the case, it postulated a groundswell that never materialized.

Quadros' supposed successor was João ("Jango") Goulart, Vice-President for the second time. A known Leftist, he was traveling in China at the time. The army kept him from returning to take over the Presidency until, with the acquiescence of a worried Congress, they had time to change the constitution once more. Goulart agreed to these changes in advance, and was allowed to return to a parliamentary system of government in which the President was supposed to be little more than a figurehead. But the structure of the Congress, with its numerous parties and personal politics, brought about kaleidoscopic changes in upper-level officials and complete failure of more conservative elements to formulate any sort of positive program.

It soon became apparent that the parliamentary system was ineffective, and Goulart gradually assumed more and more of the leadership and power in the country. He was finally strong enough to hold a national plebiscite in which the electorate voted for a return to the presidential system of government, thereby indirectly endorsing his political policies. Goulart managed for a while to keep both labor and business reasonably content to sit out the remainder of his term, since in actual fact he instituted no fundamental changes in Brazil's economic or social environment. Discontent mounted, however, as an inflated bureaucracy, spiraling inflation, and financial mistrust abroad sapped the country's economic vitality. There was also a minor international flare-up with the United States when Goulart bestowed Brazil's highest decoration on Cuba's Che Guevara, Fidel Castro's former associate who was finally killed, in October 1967, while leading a Communist guerilla band in Bolivia.

Goulart finally overstepped himself when he supported a non-commissioned officers' revolt in the Rio de Janeiro barracks. The Army's top brass, fearing the collapse of military discipline and with it, by their reasoning, the only organized opposition to Communism remaining in Brazil, marched on Rio and Brasília with reliable units from São Paulo and Minas Gerais. In this move they had the support of the Conservatives in Congress and most of the state governors. Except for some ineffective civilian protest marches and a few short-lived and largely opportunistic harassments by small guerilla bands of ex-soldiers in the interior, the Goulart regime was overthrown without opposition. The ex-President and his closest political allies were forced to flee the country.

Humberto de Alencar Castelo Branco, an army marshal, was installed in March, 1964, as interim President. Unlike previous military interventions in the affairs of state, and contrary to the usual Brazilian tolerance toward unorthodox or unpopular individual views, the new power hierarchy took a hard line against the opposition. Thousands were jailed, high officials were banished, government functionaries were dismissed, and groups that opposed the military take-over were persecuted. These measures were ostensibly aimed at Communists or those who supported them; but as has inevitably happened elsewhere with similar pogroms, the dragnet soon spread to include many against whom the charges were often unproved and frequently unbelievable, including liberal members of the church hierarchy. Among those exiled was former President Kubitschek, who was placed on a list of those prohibited from holding public office.

On the positive side, the Castelo Branco regime did put some order into the bureaucratic chaos that had steadily worsened during the preceding decade. It at least partly succeeded in curbing the rampant inflation, although continued rises in the prices of basic necessities left the urban working classes, already discontented over the summary treatment accorded many of their leaders, unenthusiastic over the new government's supposed accomplishments. In another area, Castelo Branco was responsible for drafting an agrarian reform law—based upon the graded taxation of holdings over 50 acres according to size, fertility, operational efficiency, and access to communications—which, if carried out, could be the first meaningful step toward undercutting the traditionally privileged position of the owners of large unproductive estates. He also attempted to give long-range direction to national and regional development programs through a Ten-Year Plan for Economic and Social Development. This was aimed especially at improving the nation's statistical machinery, coordinating government and private investment programs, upgrading transport systems to better meet the needs of the national economy, and promoting the growth of the petroleum, steel, and electrical industries. The Castelo Branco government also did much to improve Brazil's foreign relations, which had become chaotic. Emphasis was placed on strengthening economic relationships with the nations of the Western Hemisphere, particularly through greater integration with the markets of other Latin American countries and through bilateral agreements with the United States.

There are certain parallels between the Castelo Branco takeover and that of Getúlio Vargas a generation earlier: both removed an elected government through armed revolt; both were based on an alliance between the armed forces and conservative politicians; both were brought to a head by economic crises, a depression in one instance and inflation and a stagnant economy in the other;

and both originated from a more fundamental reaction against new political forces growing out of changed economic alignments in the East. In 1930 the reaction was in opposition to the emergent capitalist structures of São Paulo's coffee and industrial hierarchy; in 1964 it was against the ballot box strength of an electorate dominated by the urban working classes.

Yet the political realism of both men led them, in seeming contradiction, to seek support from the very interests they were apparently trying to replace, the counterpart for Vargas' P.T.B. being Castelo Branco's National Renovating Alliance (*Aliança Renovadora Nacional,* or ARENA). In the end, however, neither was willing to rely on normal electoral processes for support, and both doctored the machinery of state to suit their purposes. Vargas dissolved Congress; Castelo Branco purged it of dissidents (he also abolished all existing political parties, later permitting candidates screened by government-appointed electoral judges to form an official opposition party, the Brazilian Democratic Movement, *Movimento Democrático Brasileiro*). Vargas wrote the new Constitutions of 1933 and 1937; Castelo Branco pushed one through his rump Congress in January, 1967. Among other things, the latter changed the name of the country from the United States of Brazil to simply Brazil— in recognition, no doubt, of the completed evolution toward centralism. This newest Constitution, Brazil's sixth, gave the President greater control over public finance, provided him with almost unlimited powers in matters of "national security," and changed the rules of Presidential succession to allow indirect, rather than direct, popular election.

Castelo Branco differed in one important respect from Getúlio Vargas: he did not seek to perpetuate himself in office. In October, 1966, after the MDB candidate withdrew from the race in frustration, a purged rump Congress elected as Brazil's 22nd President, the 64-year-old *gaucho* general, Artur Costa e Silva, Castelo Branco's conservative former War Minister. With the succession assured, in November, 1966, Congressional elections were held in which ARENA candidates won 304 seats against 168 for the MDB; but about one-third of the ballots cast in São Paulo and Rio de Janeiro were blank protest votes. After assuming office in March, 1967, the new President promised to "humanize" the revolution, better the lot of the poor, especially in rural areas, and return the country to full democratic principles. Although he did permit some of the political exiles, including Kubitschek, to return to Brazil, Costa e Silva has not, at the time of this writing, repealed a strict censorship law which the outgoing Congress passed as a final authoritarian gesture at the behest of Castelo Branco—who died in a plane crash in June, 1967, shortly after relinquishing the Presidency. In the final days before this law went into effect, the ever-vitriolic Carlos Lacerda, at one time an ardent supporter of the revolution, labeled it "the tomb of Brazilian democracy," and late in 1967 the country's 22 Catholic bishops joined in a denunciation of the high-handed methods still being used under Costa e Silva after two priests were arrested for distributing anti-government pamphlets. In April 1968, riots in many state capitals and Brasília followed the March 28 slaying of a student by military police during a protest against university conditions in Rio de Janeiro.

Past experience indicates, however, that the natural common sense of the Brazilian people, derived from their esteem for individual liberty and non-institutionalized democracy, will soon reassert itself. There was, after all, not inconsiderable support for and justification of the rightist coup that put Castelo Branco in power. It is just unfortunate that the zealous military mind, seeking a monolithic and ideologically correct political structure, should have felt it necessary to achieve its ends through oppressive measures. A certain amount of adjustment and unrest is to be expected of any nation, such as Brazil, in which rapid and fundamental changes are occurring within all of its institutions, and wealth and progress are as yet unevenly distributed among socioeconomic classes and disparate regions. These themes will reappear in subsequent chapters, which focus on the major regions of this giant country, now stirring vigorously out of the sleep of centuries.

3   *The South*

Wⁱᵗʰ the possible exception of urban São Paulo, the South will no doubt feel most like home to the North American or European visitor to Brazil. Here warm summer days with quick-passing thunderstorms give way to the frosts and light snows of winter. Covering the plateau and its borderlands are pine and hardwood forests interspersed with meadows; small farms and wooden houses with the steep-sloping roofs of Bavaria; vineyards and orchards and plots of grain. On the plains of Rio Grande do Sul are wheat fields and rolling grasslands; sprawling ranch houses sheltered in neat squares of poplar and eucalyptus; fat sheep and beefy cattle. Fair people of European descent walk the country roads and city streets.

Historical and physical isolation, and immigrants who arrived directly from Europe at a relatively late period in the life-span of Brazil, have given the South its unique character. But improved communications and urbanization have, especially since World War II, tended to blur these distinctions until it is easy to exaggerate, as many authors have done, the cultural differences between the South and the rest of the country and to overemphasize its "European-ness." The region is, indisputably, Brazilian. Its first settlers and many later ones came from other parts of the nation; three have returned north to become president. Florianópolis, the capital of Santa Catarina, is as much the old colonial city as any of her sisters on the northern coasts.

Opened up from São Paulo in the early years of the seventeenth century by Jesuits and *Bandeirantes* in quest of Indian labor, the region remained isolated and backward for some 200 years. Until the close of the eighteenth century there were fewer than 100,000 people of European descent in the three provinces (Rio Grande do Sul and Santa Catarina were separated from São Paulo in 1736 and 1738 respectively, Paraná not until 1853). The South was the home of scattered stockmen who supplied cattle, horses, and mules from the open range to São Paulo and the mining region, and of a few subsistence farmers and fishermen along the coast.

The first settlers to introduce a rational and more intensive form of land use to the South were Azorean immigrants who established their farms near the coast between Santa Catarina Island and the Lagoa dos Patos. They were followed by German immigrants who, from the 1820's to the 1870's, occupied the valleys along the edge of the Serra do Mar and the Serra Geral. Then came the Italians, most of whom settled near the rim of the Southern Plateau, beyond the fringe of earlier colonization. Starting in the last decade of the nineteenth century, people from Poland and Russia moved into the central section of the plateau, between the pine forest and the prairie, filling in the area between the European small farmers and the cattle-raising Brazilians. The Slavs brought with them from eastern Europe the four-wheeled covered wagon, which was adopted throughout the Southern Plateau as the basic means of transport and continues to add charm to its country lanes.

On its periphery the South merges with other of Brazil's regions. Along the coast are isolated and poverty-stricken communities ekeing out an existence by fishing from dugout canoes and culti-vating small plots in the tropical jungle. In northern Paraná large coffee plantations are little more than extensions of those in São Paulo. And the pioneer lands of the western hardwood forests can scarcely be distinguished from those in Mato Grosso or Goiás, with their clearings littered by fallen trees and charred stumps, their hastily thrown together villages, and the bright gashes of their newly bulldozed roads reaching out to the seemingly endless horizon—a horizon which has, nevertheless, contracted palpably under the steady influx of new farming populations during this century.

A RURAL ECONOMY

The South is basically rural in its attitudes as well as in the way its people live. Of the region's total population of 14.5 million, nearly 9 million are rural. Compared to the national average according to the 1960 census, which classified 54.9 percent of the Brazilian population as rural, the figures for the three southern states were as follows: Rio Grande do Sul, 55.1 percent; Santa Catarina, 67.6 percent; and Paraná, 69 percent.

The general level of prosperity of the farmers in the South is measurably above that of their fellows in most of the rest of the country. Constituting one-fifth of Brazil's ranchers and farmers, they collectively enjoy one-third of the country's agricultural income. Rio Grande do Sul, with 3.1 percent of Brazil's land area and 7.6 percent of its population, has 7.7 percent of its rural population and 13.3 percent of its agricultural income. Santa Catarina, with 1.1 and 3.0 percent of the nation's land and population, respectively, has 3.7 percent of its farm and ranchland population, who receive 4.8 percent of the national income from those occupations. Paraná has 2.3 percent of the country's land, 6.3 percent of its population, 7.6 percent of its rural dwellers, and 15.0 percent of its income from agricultural pursuits. The farmers of the South operate one-third of Brazil's tractors and one-half of its plows, own one-third of its silos, and have available to them nearly one-half of the nation's cold storage and warehousing facilities.

From the South comes nearly all of Brazil's wheat, soybeans, *mate,* and grapes, as well as about half of its coffee, tobacco, and beans. Over one-quarter of the production of those Brazilian dietary staples, rice and cassava, is in the South. There are, of course, regional differences in agricultural production, in part because of favorable local physical conditions, but also because of the knowledge or preferences of a particular group of settlers. This is true also of livestock production: Rio Grande do Sul provides the nation with virtually all of its domestic wool, Santa Catarina has its greatest number of ducks and geese, and together the two states produce two-thirds of Brazil's hams. Some further details concerning the most important of these specialty areas are necessary for a full appreciation of the agricultural and stockraising variety that characterizes the landscape of the three southern states.

THE COFFEE BORDERLAND

Chapter 1 mentioned the fact that the occurrence of frequent, even though usually light, frosts along the northern boundary of the sub-tropical climate region on the Southern Plateau determines the poleward limit of coffee growing in Brazil. The crop is, therefore, limited on the south to northwestern Paraná. But even here cold air drainage into the valley bottoms at night increases the probability of frost, so that the lower lands are left in pasture, and coffee is planted only on the divides.

Periodic outbreaks of exceptionally cold masses of polar air, with temperatures dropping as low as 20° Fahrenheit, occur about once every ten years, however, and may "burn" many if not all of the groves as far north as the deep valleys along the São Paulo border. In 1953 over 200 million trees were "burned" by frost, and two years later the most severe temperatures ever to hit northern Paraná left the coffee groves entirely leafless. Not only were the growers in serious financial difficulties, but foreign exchange losses brought on a national economic crisis; and in the United States there was such consumer resentment against the sharp rise in coffee prices that a delegation of housewives actually went to Paraná to personally verify the damage caused. Again in 1963 a cold wave damaged half the trees and caused the loss of 60 percent of that year's harvest.

Coffee growing in northwestern Paraná is a seemingly speculative proposition, quite out of keeping with the agricultural conservatism of the rest of the South. Nevertheless, income obtained during normal years more than compensates for occasional unremunerative ones. This is because of the favorable combination of a normally ideal climate and fertile *terra roxa* soils, which produce high yields of good quality exportable coffee. Profits are also high because the cost of clearing the land and planting the coffee is returned by growing grain or other crops between the rows during the first three years before the trees begin to bear. Furthermore, the financial position of the landowners assures long-range agricultural stability. The coffee plantations have sufficient capital to tide them over one or two adverse years. On the small holding, mixed cropping (grain, fruit, and cotton) and livestock raising assure the farmer of some cash income even during years that may be catastrophic for coffee. It is sufficient to point out that northwestern Paraná continues to grow about one-half of Brazil's coffee and that although its rural population density is equaled only in a few impoverished parts of the Northeast's humid coast, the farmers of the Paraná coffee region have the highest standard of living of any rural group in the country.

Unfortunately, the Paraná coffee growers' prosperity has been derived, in part, at public expense thanks to a government price support policy, mentioned in the preceding chapter, which dates back to depression times when coffee production was centered in São Paulo. Thus, in 1966 the government was forced to spend US $260 million to buy up that year's 12 million bag surplus and warehouse it, bringing the total stockpile of surplus coffee to 65 million bags, the equivalent of about two years' total Brazilian production. In an attempt to reduce coffee production to an amount corresponding roughly to the absorptive capacity of national and international markets, in September, 1966, the government began a campaign to uproot excess trees, indemnifying the growers at a variable rate up to between 11 and 12 cents (US) per tree. Ultimately about one-half of Brazil's 2.6 billion trees will be destroyed, at a relatively modest cost of US $70 million. This will reduce coffee production by 18 percent only, since the best groves will remain. As the rate of indemnification is highest when the land is replanted, about half of the more than one million acres already cleared has been put into other crops. Since most of the eradication has taken place in Minas Gerais and Espírito Santo States, and in those areas of Paraná which produced a lower grade of coffee, the prosperous farmers of the latter state should benefit from this program, as the quality coffee grower is assured of a rational outlet for his production, and his more marginal neighbor turns to those crops for which his lands are eminently suited and for which Brazil's rapidly growing population and rising standard of living provide an ever-increasing demand.

THE SMALL HOLDER

On the outer margins of the sub-tropical climate, in the low-lying plains and valleys that fringe the Southern Plateau, there are certain areas where land occupancy patterns resemble those generally found elsewhere in Brazil. More sparsely settled than the rest of the South, they were occupied at an early date by migrants from other parts of the country. They are distinguished particularly by the continued practice of land rotation, or shifting cultivation, instead of the rotation of crops and pastures in the fashion of those farmers who are the descendents of colonists of direct and relatively recent European origins. Basically oriented toward subsistence rather than commercial agriculture, these fringe areas grow corn and cassava as the principal crops in clearings in the hardwood forests.

There are, however, certain agricultural specialties which distinguish each of these marginal areas from the others. In the western valleys the primary source of income is the cutting and curing, over open fires, of *mate,* a tea native to this part of South America. It is the basic beverage of both the Brazilian and Spanish *gaucho.* In the northeastern valleys of Paraná, between the coffee region and the limits of recent European colonization north of Curitiba, some cattle are grazed as a heritage from earlier times, and hogs are raised for sale. The Paraná coastal plain has three different commercial specialty zones intermingled with the basic subsistence farming: bananas in the foothills of the Serra do Mar; sugar cane, mostly for supplying local rum distilleries, on the terraces and floodplains; and pineapples near the coast, introduced by Japanese settlers, who use old Indian shell mounds as a source of lime to add to the sandy soils. Further south, on Santa Catarina Island and the adjacent coast, the descendents of the first group of Azorean colonists and settlers from São Vicente grow some inferior coffee, augmenting their subsistence diet by fishing in the coastal waters. In all cases, the inhabitants of these areas of traditional land rotation have significantly lower living standards than their neighbors who use more enlightened farming techniques.

The first waves of non-Portuguese immigrants to reach the South settled in the foothills of the Serra Geral north of Porto Alegre, and in the valleys that cut into the Serra do Mar in northern Santa Catarina. The mixed farming and dairying which they introduced and which subsequent immigrants also practiced with modifications has become a unique, although not universal, characteristic of the southern region. Their practice of crop rotation not only assures the continued fertility of the land, but also gives rise to a wide range of crops, producing a variety in the landscape that is seldom found in other parts of the country. This visual effect is heightened by the presence of enclosed yards, barns, sheds, and other out-buildings around steep-roofed wooden farm houses, quite unlike the appearance and simpler layout of most Brazilian farms.

The basic cropping pattern of these farms includes corn, much of which is used as hog fodder, cassava, beans, potatoes, grains, and upland rice, rotated with alfalfa and pasture grasses. *Mate* may be grown for home consumption, and there are often vineyards and small orchards containing pears, oranges, and persimmons. The proportion of land devoted to any one of these products—and, in fact, whether they appear at all—varies more with the origins and traditions of individual communities, and to a certain extent with marketing opportunities, than with differences in the physical environment. Thus, cassava is grown and milled throughout the region, the flour marketed in other parts of the country as well as locally. Vegetables, on the other hand, are grown almost entirely around the towns and cities for sale on the local market. In the belt of German colonization which extends from Curitiba to Join-ville, the sale of fresh milk is the principal cash-producing activity. Certain districts make butter and cheese, the most specialized area of cheese production being near Curitiba in colonies of pre-dominantly Dutch origins. Among farmers of Slavic origin, on the other hand, there is a preference for growing rye, oats, and barley.

On the coastal plain of Santa Catarina paddy rice is grown, particularly by colonists of Italian extraction, and here dairy cows and pigs are kept only for home consumption. In another zone of Italian settlement, along the southern rim of the plateau, wheat is an important crop and supports a number of flour mills. This last area is the center of the Brazilian wine industry, although grapes are also grown in the vicinity of Curitiba, where Italians took over their cultivation after they were introduced by French immigrants from Algeria.

Half way between Joinville and Florianópolis a tobacco-growing district supplies the cigarette factory at Blumenau, one of the earliest of the German settlements. At the other side of the plateau, on rolling sandstone hills that extend southward from the Serra Geral along the outer margin of the small-holder region of the South, tobacco is the principal crop. Here, at Santa Cruz, are Brazil's largest cigarette manufacturers (in 1965 the most important tobacco company, which has plants in other areas as well, con-tributed nearly 11 percent of the federal government's total tax revenue; it's leading cigarette ranks ninth among the world's most consumed brands). The land in this area is rather dry, and much of it is left as cattle pasture or planted in eucalyptus groves, the wood from which is used in the tobacco curing sheds. Large proper-ties are now mixed with the small ones, and to the west and south the former become the dominant occupancy feature of the Rio Grande do Sul Plains.

THE LARGE PROPERTIES

The undulating plains of southern Rio Grande do Sul, once a sea of natural grasses, are most often pictured in terms of their cattle herding traditions, of the *estancia* and the *gaucho*—and it is interesting to note that the Spanish words are used here in place of the Portuguese *fazenda* and *vaqueiro* common to the rest of Brazil. While the ranch and the cowboy are still very much in evidence and the state is the nation's second in beef production, cattle are no longer in the commanding economic position of a generation or two ago. Thus, in 1962, the 24 billion *cruzeiro* value of Rio Grande's beef industry was surpassed by that of its rice crop, which was worth 27 billion *cruzeiros,* making that state Brazil's leading producer of rice with 16 percent of the total national production. Wool and wheat production, at 22 and 21 billion *cruzeiros* respectively, almost equaled the value of beef and are far more important in the national picture, 99 percent of the country's wool and 74 percent of its wheat coming from Rio Grande do Sul.

The legacy of a past when vast land grants were parceled out as ranches persists in today's land ownership pattern in southern Rio Grande do Sul. Here large estates, whether agricultural or livestock, are very different from the small holdings to the north. The nature of farming practices also changes. For instance, the large-scale, mechanized and chemically fertilized rice farms on the lowlands west of the Lagoa dos Patos and along the flood plain of the Jacuí River are in strong contrast to the traditional small family rice plots of Santa Catarina.

Extensive commercial wheat production has gradually pushed into the former grazing area south and west of the Jacuí Valley since the 1940's. This expansion was stimulated by the shortages of World War II, by subsequent import and milling restrictions aimed at reducing the exchange drain caused by imports of flour, and by a complete overhaul of the Rio Grande do Sul road network. In 1938 the latter consisted of only 260 miles of all-weather roads and a collection of tracks and trails which a contemporary highway congress labeled the worst communication system in Brazil except for that of Acre Territory in the upper Amazon. Today, thanks to the improvement of existing highways and the building of many new ones, Rio Grande do Sul is surpassed only by São Paulo and Guanabara States in the number of vehicles in circulation. The great strides that have been taken in recent years to better communications in all three of the southern states have enabled them to approach the realization of their full potential as efficient producers of high-quality agricultural products. It is in this role that the South will undoubtedly continue to fulfill its most useful function in the Brazilian economy.

URBANIZATION AND INDUSTRIALIZATION

Manufacturing in the three southern states of Brazil falls almost entirely into two categories: making consumer goods for local or regional markets and processing raw materials from the land for national or, in some cases, international distribution. Wheat, rice, and cassava milling have been mentioned among the latter group, to which also belong the meat packing plants and tanneries by the Lagoa dos Patos, the cigarette factories of Santa Cruz and Blumenau, and the wine distilleries of the Serra Geral. The timber-using industries of the pine forests belong to both categories, and Paraná is Brazil's leading state in timber and lumber production, with Santa Catarina in third place and Rio Grande do Sul in fourth.

As for consumer-oriented industries, the high living standards and purchasing power of the rural population, as well as the doubling of the urban population in each of the past two decades, have provided good markets for such industries as foodstuffs, beverages, clothing, and furniture. Rio Grande do Sul holds third place in the national production of the last three items, as well as second place in the first, followed by Paraná. Rio Grande do Sul is also the third state of Brazil in the manufacture of chemicals and fourth in metallurgy, the center of which is Porto Alegre, where seaborne mineral imports come closest to the small coal deposits of the Jacuí Valley and the Laguna district.

In some cases, specialty items have developed out of the skills of immigrant craftsmen. Curitiba, for example, makes barrels for the *mate* industry because a barrel-maker from Germany happened to settle there. The inlaid wood products which are highly regarded in the gift and souvenir trades, were first made in that city for similar reasons. At Caxias do Sul a tiny frame house, the first workshop of the metalsmith Abramo Eberle, now perches nostalgically atop a multi-storied factory which produces stainless steel and silver cutlery, sheath knives, riding paraphernalia, and most of the high quality decorated gourds and *bombillas,* or hollow spoons—prerequisites for the proper brewing and drinking of *mate* —used by the *gauchos* of both Brazil and the La Plata countries.

Based on such a variety of manufacturing and processing enterprises, the South has 20 percent of Brazil's industrial establishments and employs 16 percent of its industrial labor force, with the implication that plants are modern and the work force efficient. On the other hand, because the principal industrial activities involve the processing of raw materials, especially of relatively low value foodstuffs and timber, the value added by manufacturing in the South amounts to only 13 percent of the national total, with the final value of the goods produced constituting but 11 percent of the country's industrial income. Nevertheless, with its firmly based agricultural economy, a highly skilled and well educated people, and the diversification and new opportunities being brought about by an urbanizing population, the South should continue to be one of the most prosperous and well-balanced sections of Brazil.

In the past quarter of a century, somnolent southern villages have become bustling cities; and the two leading cities, Porto Alegre and Curitiba, have become modern metropolises. The former, which looks like a small Manhattan from the air, has over 800,000 inhabitants and ranks fifth among the nation's urban centers. With more cars per capita than any other city in the country, Porto Alegre has been called by its famed author, Erico Verissimo, "the most middle-class capital of Brazil." Curitiba, which was founded in the early decades of the seventeenth century by *Bandeirantes* returning from forays against the Jesuit Indian missions along the Paraná and Uruguay Rivers, remained for many years little more than a market town serving a local farm area, in spite of being the state capital.

In 1940 it had a population of only 70,000. Today Curitiba is a thriving metropolis of half a million inhabitants, often referred to as the "small São Paulo" because of its location near the rim of the escarpment, its rapid growth as a regional manufacturing center, and its dynamic modernity. Curitiba exemplifies the changes and progress that have taken place in Brazil in recent years, sparked by the development of the East.

4   *The East*

THAT region known in Brazilian statistical par-
lance as the East,[1] is the only one which fails to find an historic
definition in the regional folklore and spirit of the country. Made
up of *Paulistas* and *Cariocas, Capichabas* and *Mineiros,* it includes
the states of São Paulo, Rio de Janeiro, Guanabara (the tiny former
Federal District that consists of little more than the city of Rio de
Janeiro), Espírito Santo, and Minas Gerais.

Although the East has only one-tenth (10.8 percent) of the
national area, it contains over two-fifths (43.3 percent) of the
Brazilian people. In this region are most of Brazil's railroads and
highways, the preponderance of its industries, and the headquarters of its strongest labor unions and political parties. It contains over one-half of Brazil's urban population (55.5 percent) and
large cities—that is, 13 of the 24 that have over 200,000 inhabitants
(Map 3)—and two of the four principal metropolitan centers in
Latin America, São Paulo and Rio de Janeiro.

The East is the most progressive and wealthy section of the
country. Yet it is also the traditional home of the *caiçara,* isolated
fisherman and subsistence farmer; of his neighbor the *caipira,* hillbilly of the coastal mountains; of the *garimpeiro,* or prospector;
and of the *vaqueiro,* cowboy of the remote cattle regions. Here live
fabulously wealthy business tycoons of the modern Western World
as well as millions of *favelados,* those desperately poor shantytown

1 The boundaries, and even the name of the East, or *Leste,* have been
changed on several occasions in official statistical presentations of census data.

54

dwellers who appear to be an inevitable element in every Latin American city today.

Better than any other of Brazil's regions, the East illustrates the optimistic dynamism of modern Latin America in conflict with the despair engendered by outmoded institutions. In this conflict is the mainspring of hope for future growth and development; but the hope is often nullified by the unsuccessful use of existing physical and human resources. Where the other, peripheral, regions of Brazil may find their key in physical and historical unity, the East can be understood only in terms of its disharmonies, contradictions, and conflicts. Yet these factors may, in themselves, have stimulated the region's growth patterns.

HIGHLAND AND COASTAL METROPOLISES

One of these conflicts has always existed between the East's two primary physical divisions, the highland and the coast. During the past few decades, attention has been strikingly focused on this dichotomy during the battle for economic and political supremacy between the cities of Rio de Janeiro and São Paulo, in which the latter won an important round with the transfer of the capital from Rio to Brasília.

This division extends back to the earliest days of Portuguese penetration and settlement, to the time when the lowlands around Guanabara Bay were given over to a sugar plantation economy oriented toward, and dependent upon, Europe, while the self-sufficient *Bandeirantes* of the São Paulo plateau were roaming the backlands of the Paraguay-Paraná and Amazon drainage basins. However, as long as Brazil depended upon the export of raw materials—sugar, gold, and coffee—for its well-being and as long as it was content to trade these products with Europe for all but its bare necessities, Rio de Janeiro continued to dominate not only the East, but Brazil as a whole, of which it was the primary commercial center.

Table 2 shows the different growth rates of the two modern cities —Rio de Janeiro on the coast and São Paulo on the plateau—since

TABLE 2

Growth of the Cities

| | Population | |
Year	Rio de Janeiro	São Paulo
1808	100,000	20,000
1890	500,000	70,000
1920	1,200,000	600,000
1936	1,700,000	1,200,000
1950	2,300,000	2,200,000
1960	3,200,000	3,900,000
1967	4,000,000	5,500,000

Brazil's emergence from colonial status. São Paulo lagged well behind Rio throughout the commercial period of exporting unprocessed agricultural products. But in both cases significant growth (i.e., to populations of about half a million) was first realized when the coffee plantations established dense rural settlements in the respective hinterlands of each and began to send to the cities an unprecedented flow of wealth. In Rio the process took place during the Empire (1822–1889), based on the slave estates of the Paraíba Valley. In São Paulo, which city still had only 26,000 residents in 1872, rapid growth occurred during the quarter century between emancipation and World War I, when the population of the state trebled (1.4 to 4.6 million) as immigrants from abroad and from other parts of the country came to work as tenants on the coffee plantations of the plateau. Subsequent expansion to and beyond the one million mark resulted as each city evolved commercial and industrial functions appropriate to fulfilling wider regional and national roles.

SÃO PAULO—FOCUS OF MODERN PROSPERITY

Today, São Paulo State has 18 percent of Brazil's people, but only 3 percent of its area. Within its boundaries are 17 percent of the country's cultivated land and 11 percent of its agricultural workers. Many of these farmers have progressed beyond their early status as tenants on the all-encompassing coffee plantations, and now produce a great variety of crops that account for 27 percent of the nation's farm income. By value, São Paulo produces 99 percent of Brazil's silk, 95 percent of its peanuts, half of its sugar and tomatoes, about one-third of its cotton, potatoes, ham, beef, and grapes, and approximately one-fourth of its coffee, rice, castor beans, oranges, pineapples, milk, and chickens. São Paulo is also the leading banana producing state, with nearly 20 percent of that crop. This agricultural productivity is not unrelated to the fact that 44 percent of the nation's tractors operate within its boundaries.

São Paulo's prosperity and the remarkable growth of its capital city have come not just from the sale of agricultural products, but from the establishment of industries based upon the processing of these and other raw materials. At the same time, increasingly prosperous rural and urban communities (the state today contains one-fourth of all Brazil's urban population) have been able to buy back the locally produced manufactures and to support an increasing number of services. This process was facilitated by the availability of a large body of skilled immigrants, who provided the technical and entrepreneurial know-how, and also by the investment of profits from coffee in diverse productive enterprises. Unlike their counterparts of slave plantation days, whose primary motivation was self-gratification, the owners of the São Paulo coffee *fazendas* reinvested their profits in the land, in businesses within the towns where they had established roots, and in manufacturing establishments in the larger cities.

Much of this wealth was concentrated in the city of São Paulo. So were the energies of a new breed of businessmen and manufacturers. The location of the city near the rim of the escarpment gave it access to an internal trade area across the plateau as large as all of Argentina, and oceanic access through the port of Santos to markets along the Brazilian coast and abroad. In a few decades, this combination of factors enabled São Paulo City to rise to preeminence among the manufacturing centers of Latin America.

The original, basically internal orientation of São Paulo's industrial growth is illustrated by the fact that during the depression, when stagnation and unemployment racked the major industrial nations of the world, São Paulo increased its production of steel from 4,000 to 22,000 tons, of cement from 100,000 to 250,000 tons, and of cotton fibers from 15,000 to 200,000 tons. Thus was formed a solid base for the subsequent evolution of the metallurgical, construction, and textile industries. The fastest rate of growth came between 1940 and 1950 because of wartime shortages and accumulated monetary surpluses after the war; during this period the number of industrial establishments in São Paulo State rose from 6,700 to 23,300. A particularly high growth rate was shown in textiles and clothing (from 800 to 3,000 establishments, compared with 6,500 today) and in the metallurgical, mechanical, and electrical industries, which quadrupled during that decade from 500 plants to 2,000, then trebled in the next 15 years to 6,000.

By 1965 the number of manufacturing establishments in the state had increased to 45,500 and industrial employment had risen to over a million workers—more people than are found in the entire state of Amazonas. In that year São Paulo State had 38 percent of Brazil's factories, which accounted for 60 percent of the total value of the country's industrial production. This included over 90 percent of the mechanical and rubber industries' production, by value, and 88 percent of that of the communications and transport industries. Nearly 60 percent of all the trucks, busses, and automobiles now operating in Brazil have been nationally made, and of the 13 plants that produce them 11 are in metropolitan São Paulo.[2] One-third of the country's motor vehicles, and a quarter of the paved roads, are in São Paulo State. The building up of the automotive and other industries has attracted three-fourths of Brazil's foreign investments during the past ten years to São Paulo State, over 50 percent going into the metropolitan area.

[2] In 1957, when the industry was established, there were only 800,000 motor vehicles in Brazil. Today there are 1.5 million passenger cars alone on the road—a third more than in the Soviet Union, which has three times the population—and the ratio of people-to-cars has dropped from 81 to 38, while São Paulo State's 22 persons per car is surpassed only in Guanabara.

GREATER SÃO PAULO, PRODUCTIVE HEARTLAND

The greatest industrial and commercial concentration within São Paulo State is in its capital city and the 37 surrounding municipalities that together constitute Greater São Paulo. Here 46 percent of the state's manufacturing establishments produce 69 percent of the value of its industrial output, corresponding figures for the city proper being 37 and 44 percent. Greater São Paulo has over 20,000 plants which employ about 650,000 workers—39 percent of the Brazilian industrial labor force—and account for nearly half the country's total industrial production, by value. As might be supposed from the high value of their output in relation to the state and the nation, all but 10 percent of Greater São Paulo's industrial workers are in skilled, technical, or managerial jobs, about half of them being employed in the four leading industries (textiles, transport equipment, metallurgy, and electrical and communications products).

High value industrial production finds its parallel in agriculture, as Greater São Paulo also produces 92 percent of the state's lettuce, 78 percent of its cabbages, two-thirds of its cauliflowers, and over half of its sweet potatoes, persimmons, and peaches. This market gardening is mostly in the hands of the Japanese, of whom there are 42,000 in Greater São Paulo today, not including Brazilian-born and naturalized citizens. The Japanese are second only to the Italians in number, there being over 100,000 of the latter in the metropolitan area, followed by 50,000 Spaniards, 31,500 Germans, and 13,000 Syrians and Lebanese. There are also 40,000 immigrant Jews, mostly of German or Polish origin, 33,000 Slavs from various parts of eastern Europe and Russia, and many smaller foreign groups. By far the greater proportion of the quarter of a million newcomers who arrive each year come, however, from the interior of the state, from the Northeast, or from Minas Gerais, in that order. In the past seven years, Greater São Paulo has grown to its present population of 7 million by the addition of two million immigrants, one-and-a-half million of whom have settled in São

Paulo City. That they can all be absorbed into an expanding labor force is indicated by the fact that the Sunday edition of the newspaper *Estado de São Paulo* carries an average of thirty full pages of help-wanted ads each week.

On the other hand, such rapid growth in the metropolitan area has produced a severe strain on public services and housing, which is aggravated by the attraction of capital and skilled labor to the more lucrative manufacturing sectors. Greater São Paulo's 600,000 private cars, 30,000 taxis, and 4,000 busses move at a mean speed of 6 miles per hour, and the daily journey to and from work by this and other means of transport takes the average worker four hours. There are only 460 mailmen to deliver a quarter of a million letters a day; a chronic telephone deficit has reached 130,000 instruments; 35 percent of the people lack piped water; and 60 percent of the dwellings are not served by a sewage system. Thus far, the partial solutions of a fragmented and archaic system of public administration have been unable to cope adequately with the overall problems of organization required for the efficient functioning of a modern metropolitan area such as Greater São Paulo. It is said that the cause of relieving the city's congestion and disorganization has not been advanced by an administrative philosophy of *deixar como está para ver como fica*—leave it alone to see what happens to it.

Nevertheless, whatever the failings of its social structures, economically the city of São Paulo, with its metropolitan area, is a dynamic economic force. Furthermore, unlike such concentrations of urban productivity in most of Brazil, or for that matter in Latin America, the prosperity is reflected also in the state's smaller cities, towns, and rural areas. As a result, São Paulo State enjoys a per capita income of about US $400, higher than that of many European countries. The stimulus of this progressive center has brought benefits to producers, consumers, and investors over a very broad area.

A spectacular example of even wider benefits accruing to the nation from the development of São Paulo is the Urubupungá Dam, now under construction on the Paraná River near Três Lagoas.

Planned and built entirely by Brazilians, this 4.6 million kw hydroelectric complex will be surpassed only by the one at Krasnoyarsk in the U.S.S.R. A preliminary capacity of 1.4 million kw is expected by 1968, and when the plant is in full operation it will have played a key part in the projected doubling of Brazil's electricity production from a present 6.3 million kw to 12.5 million kw in 1972. Not only will São Paulo, which is paying nearly one-fourth of the cost of building Urubupungá directly out of its own resources, become the most electrified region in South America, but power will also be supplied to an area extending to Brasília, Corumbá, Rio de Janeiro, and Porto Alegre. Subsidiary benefits will include locks to improve shipping on the Paraná River and an estimated production of 400,000 tons of fish every year from the lakes that will be dammed up.

São Paulo's impact is being felt throughout Brazil, thanks to both the force of its evolving economy and the example of its progress. That state's increasing manufactures for national consumption and for export are easing the economic difficulties which Brazil suffered for so long as a result of being obliged to exchange low value raw materials for expensive manufactured goods from abroad. São Paulo has also provided industrial, commercial, and construction jobs for countless migrants who have come from parts of the country where progress is too slow to furnish the opportunities demanded by today's rising expectations.

This concentration of productivity in a single state is reflected in the saying that São Paulo is Brazil's locomotive pulling 21 empty cars (representing, of course, the other states). Unfortunately, one locomotive is not enough for the uphill job; and while it may be an exaggeration to say that the other cars are empty, there is no doubt that Brazil would be a far different country today if the rest of the states could equal the level of progress attained by São Paulo.

GUANABARA AND RIO DE JANEIRO

Undoubtedly the two states which come closest to São Paulo's high level of development are Guanabara and Rio de Janeiro, both inextricably linked to the fortunes of the city of Rio de Janeiro. Between them they include only 0.51 percent of the national territory, but they support nearly 10 percent of the country's population, including 16.5 percent of its urban inhabitants. Guanabara's population is 97.5 percent urban, while that of Rio de Janeiro is 61 percent.

The difference in income levels between the two states is great. In Guanabara the average annual per capita income is approximately US $1,000 (the same as for the city of São Paulo), but that of Rio de Janeiro State is only one-third as much. The latter has about 4.6 percent of the national income which, since it has 4.8 percent of the country's population, makes it about "average." Guanabara however has 13.6 percent of Brazil's total annual income going to the same approximate number of people as in Rio de Janeiro. It is interesting to note, though, that while Rio de Janeiro's share of the national income has remained constant over the past decade, that of what is now Guanabara State has dropped two percentage points (from 15.3 in 1950) during the same period. On the basis of both population (Table 2) and income, it is apparent that the relative power of the city of Rio de Janeiro within the country has, to a certain extent, declined during the past 30 years.

The growth of cities and industries in the interior and around the periphery of Rio de Janeiro City has somewhat reduced that city's predominant intellectual and material position in the country as a whole, although only its material position is subject to measurement. Thus, while the city's share of Brazilian domestic trade decreased from 23 to 22 percent between 1950 and 1960, São Paulo's increased from 25.5 to 27 percent. More important, although between 1950 and 1960 the number of Guanabara's industrial establishments showed a modest increase from 4,900 to 5,300, this was only an 8 percent growth rate and far below the overall national average of 32 percent during the same period.

In contrast, the industrial growth rate for the state of Rio de Janeiro in the same decade was 28.1 percent (from 3,500 to 4,500 establishments), which compares favorably with the national rate and São Paulo State's 31.8 percent. In part, this difference between the city's growth and the State's can be accounted for by the decentralization of the city of Rio's industries to nearby sites like Nova Iguaçu and Duque de Caxias, and by the attractions of such interior locations as Petrópolis and Volta Redonda, all of which approximately doubled their populations between 1950 and 1960. But the slow rate of expansion in the former capital is not unrelated to the problems that have arisen within Guanabara State itself or, more particularly, within the city of Rio de Janeiro.

RIO DE JANEIRO—THE "MARVELOUS" CITY

The relative slowness of recent industrial growth in Guanabara reflects the extreme overcrowding of the city of Rio de Janeiro, a gradual decline in the quality of services and amenities offered, and the presence of the federal government, which has stifled progress by the tentacular acquisitiveness of its politicians and bureaucrats, who bottle up initiative beneath red tape, graft, and sheer inertia.

In the past, Rio's physical needs had been taken care of adequately and sometimes lavishly by the application of federal funds. But as the national interest was diverted to more pressing problems, very little was done to bring the city up to date since the time Vargas slashed a broad avenue across the downtown district. Meanwhile, public and private construction went on apace, and the population soared. Whereas the 1950 census listed 58 *favelas* in Rio, with about 170,000 inhabitants, that of 1960 showed 147 shantytowns, containing a third of a million people. In the famous Copacabana residential district, which consists of a strip a few blocks wide beside a magnificient but overcrowded beach, the population increased from 75,000 in 1940, to 130,000 in 1950, and nearly 250,000 in 1960, making it the most densely populated residential area in the world. By this time, the deterioration of transport and public services had reached virtually crisis proportions in the congested, mountain-ringed "Marvelous City" (*Cidade Maravilhosa*), so-called because of its natural and architectural wonders.

It was at this point, in 1960, that the Federal District was transferred to the Central Plateau and Guanabara State was created. This solution, instead of an alternative proposal to amalgamate Rio State and the former Federal District, was undoubtedly beneficial to the city of Rio because the latter could tackle its problems without opposition from an unsympathetic hinterland or the discords and inefficiencies of a fragmented administrative apparatus, Rio being virtually Guanabara—or vice-versa. The crusading journalist Carlos Lacerda was elected the new state's first Governor. He turned out to be a dedicated, imaginative and, not unexpectedly, hard-driving administrator. Lacerda very soon doubled Guanabara's revenue from the sales tax by the simple expedient of holding a lottery based on the customers' sales slips, which they now demanded. Previously the tax had gone unpaid because sales were not recorded. Nor did he long delay in tackling the city's two most pressing problems: providing a water supply which did not require rationing and waterless days—or weeks; and organizing the transportation system so that it would move people at a faster-than-pedestrian pace around the city.

Two steps went far toward immediately unclogging Rio's congested streets. First, Lacerda banished the multitude of small private busses, or *lotações,* which not only were a danger to life and limb but also had a very low passenger to vehicle-space ratio. Second, he succeeded in enforcing no-parking regulations by letting the air out of violators' tires, a much greater deterrent to important personages than the levying of uncollectable fines. To solve longer-range problems, the Governor reverted to the city's time-honored and only practicable method of adding new trafficways: tunneling under the mountains and casting smaller hills into the bay as fill. This he did in spectacular fashion. During his term in office, from 1961 to 1965, nearly a million cubic yards of fill went into the bay. This provided space not only for multiple-lane highways, but for new beaches and enough level land to expand the parks for which Rio is famous and also for playgrounds, tracks, bandstands, restaurants, a museum, and a war memorial. To link up the new road system, 18,570 feet of new tunnels were drilled through the granite mountains—nearly twice the 9,354 feet that had been built since the first tunnel was opened in 1897.

To alleviate Rio's chronic water shortage, Lacerda's administration built an aqueduct which supplied 44 million gallons a day, increasing the available supply by 20 percent. He also began construction of what will be the largest subterranean aqueduct in the world, part of which was put in use in April, 1966. When completed, it will carry 600 million gallons of water daily through a 27-mile tunnel, meeting Rio's needs until its population reaches 8 million, which it is expected to do about the year 2000.

Despite this evidence of progress, the Lacerda government did little toward achieving a basic solution of Rio's *favela* problem. It is true that in recent years the shantytown dweller has been given some hope for a tidier future through church-sponsored apartment blocks; but this is at best a piecemeal, temporary approach to the basic social and economic question. Nevertheless, a number of such buildings have been built, the apartments being sold at cost on the installment plan, with payments calculated on the basis of the minimum wage. In some *favelas,* clinics and self-help rebuilding projects are also underway, but the task remains a monumental one.

On the fringes of the city, in both Guanabara and Rio de Janeiro states, some attention is also being given to reviving the once thriving truck farms on the alluvial soils of the Baixada Fluminense. It is hoped that this will lure some of the *favelados* back to the land as well as improve and reduce the cost of Rio's food supply. These lands have, over the years, fallen into the hands of real estate operators and speculators, who are holding them unproductively both as a hedge against inflation and as a speculative investment, anticipating the day when expansion into the suburbs will either drive up land values there or make housing developments profitable. The feasibility of any such rehousing or resettlement schemes has yet to be proven, whether in Rio de Janeiro or in other large Latin American cities, principally because of the vastness of the slum problem, whose final solution can come only through better-paying jobs for all.

The most pressing problems that must now be faced by Rio de Janeiro, whose physical needs will seemingly be cared for in the not too distant future, are in the realm of intangibles. These include a seriously unbalanced socio-economic structure; a lack of progressiveness among the elite who run its affairs; a speculative economic orientation left over from earlier times; and the eventual, if unwilling, withdrawal of the Federal Government, with its subsidies and perquisites. The at times irrationally conservative Carlos Lacerda was either unable or unwilling to cope with these problems, which must be dealt with if the modernization of Rio de Janeiro is to be more fundamental than the addition of works of engineering, important as these may be. In fact, despite the obvious progress that had been made during the preceding five years, the continued dissatisfaction of the public was expressed in the local election of 1965 with the defeat of the candidates backed by Lacerda. Whether or not future administrations of Rio de Janeiro can mobilize its resources—especially its location on a superb harbor and the rising productivity and purchasing power of its satellite towns and the neighboring interior—to make it truly the "Marvelous City" it has been in the past, only time will tell.

THE GENERALITY OF MINAS GERAIS

A rapidly expanding city in the interior is progressive, planned Belo Horizonte, capital of Minas Gerais since 1896 when it was transferred from the gold mining center at Ouro Preto. Belo Horizonte is the apex of a triangle, the other two points being at Rio de Janeiro and São Paulo, within the boundaries of which is over two-thirds of Brazil's industrial production. During the past 15 years the number of industrial establishments in the Minas capital has doubled, to over 4,000; yet this growth has not kept pace with the rate of population growth, which has doubled during the past decade. Belo Horizonte now has nearly one million inhabitants, putting it in a close race with 400-year-old Recife for Brazil's third city.

Since its founding, Belo Horizonte has had an important commercial function, at least in part due to the trading propensity of the *Mineiros,* who are sometimes said to be the New Englanders of Brazil. Their success in this field is best illustrated by the story of the Banco de Lavoura de Minas Gerais. It was founded in Belo Horizonte in 1925, when the city's population was only 50,000. The bank's first branch in the interior of the state was opened in 1930. Six years later a branch was established in Rio de Janeiro, and by 1949 the bank had branches in every Brazilian state. By 1955 it had grown to be the largest private bank in Brazil, and the following year the largest in Latin America. In 1964 when a branch was opened in New York City, the Banco de Lavoura became the first Latin American bank licensed to operate in the United States. This has, indeed, been a spectacular success story for an organization which was begun for the purpose of handling the finances of farmers in what was, a generation ago, a relatively distant and backward section of the country.

With the modernization of the state's economy, the government of Minas Gerais has encouraged the location of new industries near Belo Horizonte. One of the measures taken has been to establish industrial parks about 10 miles out of the city, to the northeast and southwest. At good power and transportation sites, the state-owned land within them is leased in perpetuity to national or foreign manufacturing enterprises at very low rates.

The present attraction of the city owes much to its location near raw materials, both mineral and agricultural, and to suitable transportation. Minas Gerais, which contains 7 percent of Brazil's area, has 22 percent of the country's railroad trackage, amounting to 5,300 miles. Whereas most of these rails were laid many decades ago, Minas Gerais had practically no paved roads before 1956, when Juscelino Kubitschek, the former governor of that state, assumed the presidency. With a combination of federal and state highway funds, paved roads were built linking Belo Horizonte to Rio de Janeiro in 1957 and to São Paulo in 1960. Between 1960 and

1962, the last year for which figures are available, the state increased its total road network from about 30,000 to 45,000 miles, more effectively linking the capital to outlying districts.

A further stimulus to economic development in recent years, not only at the capital but throughout the state, has been the rapidly increasing production of hydroelectric power. A number of modest projects make use of the many water courses which originate in the rugged topography of Minas Gerais, which contains no known deposits of coal or petroleum. Worthy of special note, however, is the giant Furnas Dam in the southern part of the state. Built between 1958 and 1965, it has a capacity of 1.2 million kw, which makes it the largest dam operating in South America. In the western part of the state, where the demand for electricity has been increasing at an annual rate of 20 percent, capacity will be doubled within the next five years with the construction of a 600,000 kw hydroelectric plant, also on the Rio Grande.

The traditional foundation of the Minas economy is, however, farming. The state's large volume of farm production comes mostly from the once-forested southeastern and southwestern parts; whereas animal husbandry and subsistence farming occupy most of the central and northern sections. The continued importance of commercial farming in Minas Gerais is due both to its better-than-average soils, located particularly in the southwesternmost part known as the "Minas Triangle," and to the hard work of its people, who are still for the most part using traditional methods.

The fact is that Minas has not been able to keep pace agriculturally with other parts of the country, notably São Paulo and the South, where mechanization has taken place; and its share of Brazil's farm income dropped from 19.3 percent in 1950 to 16.3 percent in 1960. This income was received by only 13 percent of Brazil's farmers tilling 12 percent of its cultivated land; but that fact does not obscure the difficulty in which the state finds itself, with only 8 percent of the nation's tractors and 9 percent of its plows. The small scale of operations is indicated by the phenomenon of Minas' having more than one-fourth of all the silos in the country, yet only 4 percent of the total volume of storage capacity. Diversification is the key to the continued importance of farming in Minas Gerais: it produces one-third of Brazil's milk and between 15 and 20 percent of its corn, beans, rice, pineapples, chickens, horses, mules, cattle, and hogs; it also accounts for about one-tenth of the nation's production of coffee, tobacco, potatoes, oranges, bananas, honey, ducks, and geese.

Within the state's economy, income from agriculture dropped from 50 percent of the total in 1950 to 47 percent in 1960, which was nearly balanced by the rise from 15 to 17.5 percent of the industrial sector. But while this reflected an increase in the total number of industrial establishments from 10,000 to 12,000, it did not improve Minas Gerais' share of the national plant. Unfortunately, more recent figures have not been published, but it may be assumed that Minas has considerably bettered its position in the industrial picture of the country in recent years. This is particularly true with respect to factories making higher-value finished products, as in 1960 most of the industries of that state involved the lower-value, first stage processing of raw materials. Thus, although Minas Gerais had 11 percent of Brazil's industrial establishments and 8 percent of its industrial employees, it accounted for only 6 percent of the nation's industrial income.

A true measure of the significance of Minas Gerais is, however, as the mining heart of Brazil. The importance of its gold, diamonds, and semi-precious stones recedes before the diversity of its yield of ores that are needed as a basis for modern industrial development. In total, Minas accounts for 68 percent of the nation's mineral production, much of it coming from the highly mineralized zone to the south and east of Belo Horizonte. The state produces 99 or more percent of the country's iron ore, nickel, bauxite, and graphite, and over 90 percent of its mica and beryllium. From Minas also come half of Brazil's rock crystal and dolomite and between one-fourth and one-third of its cassiterite, talc, marble, lime, and cement. Until recently 90 percent of Brazil's manganese came from Minas Gerais, but this has dropped to 14 percent with the mining of new deposits in Amapá. Whether or not new and competing deposits of some or even most of these minerals are discovered in other parts of the country, it is very doubtful that any region will be able to compete with Minas Gerais in its fortuitous juxtaposition of such a variety of minerals, which should gain increasing importance with the upgrading of Brazil's industrial complex.

THE RIO DOCE VALLEY AND VITÓRIA

One of the most promising areas for future development in Minas Gerais, and in the country, lies in the valley of the Rio Doce, the natural yet long-neglected passageway between the coast and the metallurgical zone. As long ago as the early 1800's, the well-known traveler Saint-Hilaire suggested this as the best route over the Serra do Mar, even though the river is not navigable beyond the edge of the coastal plain. It was not, however, until 1930 that a railroad was built along the Rio Doce connecting Minas Gerais to the port of Vitória, for exporting timber and iron ore from the middle reaches of the valley.

Then, during the 1940's, a number of significant changes took place within the area. First, the Rio-Bahia road was completed. Although it was not paved until 1963, it provided north-south accessibility as well as an artery from which side roads could be extended into the unoccupied highlands north of the Rio Doce. This led to the clearing of large areas of forest and the establishment of new coffee plantations and pastures for fattening cattle. At the same time, the quality and load capacity of the railroad were improved, and the iron mining activities in the valley were consolidated under the Companhia Vale do Rio Doce.

In the late 1940's a steel plant was built in the valley by a company now controlled by the Cia. Vale do Rio Doce. Using hydroelectric power and locally produced charcoal, it was located at Coronel Fabriciano, near Governador Valadares and not far from Brazil's vast "Iron Mountain," Itabira. By 1963 the Coronel Fabriciano plant attained an annual production of 120,000 tons of high grade steel. In that same year production began in the Usina

Siderúrgica de Minas Gerais plant at Monlevade, further up the Rio Doce Valley about 50 miles from Belo Horizonte. Approximately 40 percent of its capital was of Japanese origin. Production at this plant is now 500,000 tons a year, which compares favorably with the million and a quarter tons capacity of the twenty-year-old Volta Redonda mill between Rio de Janeiro and São Paulo. Already the largest plate mill in Latin America, Monlevade as it expands production will be of utmost importance to Brazil's automobile, oil, and shipbuilding industries. Monlevade is expected to produce two and a half million tons of steel a year by 1980 (when Volta Redonda's production should be about three and a half million tons), with an eventual capacity on the order of six million tons.

The impact not only of these but also of other enterprises like lumber and furniture factories, packing plants, and repair shops, all of which are associated with the development of transportation in the Rio Doce Valley, has been reflected in a high rate of population increase within the region. For instance, in the rural Serra dos Aimorés, a portion of the Serra do Mar that has for some years been the object of a border dispute between Minas Gerais and Espírito Santo, the population increased from 67,000 in 1940 to 150,000 in 1950 and 385,000 in 1960. Governor Valadares, the commercial center of the Rio Doce Valley and the fastest growing city in Minas, was a village of only 3,000 inhabitants in 1940; by 1950 it had reached 20,000, while the figure stood at 70,000 in the 1960 census and may well be twice that today. With balanced resources for mining, logging, farming, grazing, and manufacturing backed up by a large and easily developable hydroelectric potential, the evolution of the Rio Doce Valley's economy has just begun.

The natural outlet for much of the production from the Rio Doce is the port of Vitória, capital of Espírito Santo State, on a harbor that resembles a smaller version of Guanabara Bay. With a population of about 85,000 the city has not, however, exhibited the growth that its location at an important gateway to the interior might suggest. This long-standing failure to expand can be attributed primarily to two facts: the generally conservative nature of those who control its destinies and its failure to become more than a trans-shipment point for the export of unprocessed raw materials from the interior. Vitória has attracted few local manufactures, and thereby languishes in pre-industrial torpor, although a small government steel mill was built there recently.

A subsidiary port has recently been opened ten kilometers south of the city, at Tubarão. Whether this will induce greater development at Vitória is problematical, as the primary goal of that project was simply to increase the volume of iron ore exports to 35 million tons annually, about three times the previous rate. A portion of these exports will be shipped in two new, 104,000 ton ore carriers and tankers ordered by the Cia. Vale do Rio Doce for delivery in 1970; costing US $9.3 million each, they represent the largest Latin American order ever placed in a Japanese shipyard. The principal benefits of Tubarão will undoubtedly be felt in the interior, particularly in the Rio Doce Valley—a situation which is very much in keeping with the trend that exists throughout Brazil's East: to use its rapidly growing productivity for raising the standard of living of its own people.

MORE THAN ONE LOCOMOTIVE

In summation, the East may be considered a region of great diversity in resources, in economic development, and in social organization. The fastest growing and richest section of the country, with its biggest cities, largest factories, and highest living standards, it nevertheless includes pockets of backwardness, some of which date back to Brazil's colonial era and some of which are a product of the growing-pains of modernization. However, as the nation turns ever more in upon itself, drawing upon its own resources for the good of its people, there is no doubt that these areas will at least to some degree be brought up to date through better transportation, more job opportunities, and fundamental social and economic changes. Much of such a transformation is already in the process of realization in the East.

More than any other region, the East functions on the basic

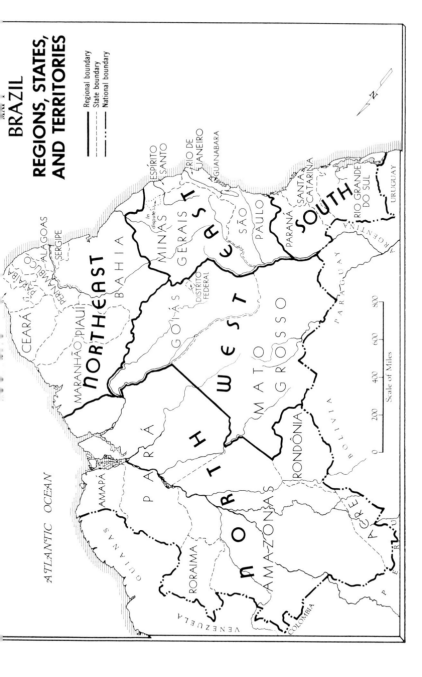

MAP 1

BRAZIL
REGIONS, STATES, AND TERRITORIES

———— Regional boundary
------- State boundary
-··-··- National boundary

NORTHEAST

EAST

WEST

SOUTH

NORTH

ATLANTIC OCEAN

CEARÁ
MARANHÃO
PIAUÍ
PARAÍBA
PERNAMBUCO
ALAGOAS
SERGIPE
BAHIA
ESPÍRITO SANTO
MINAS GERAIS
RIO DE JANEIRO
GUANABARA
SÃO PAULO
PARANÁ
SANTA CATARINA
RIO GRANDE DO SUL
GOIÁS
DISTRITO FEDERAL
MATO GROSSO
RONDÔNIA
PARÁ
AMAPÁ
GUIANAS
RORAIMA
AMAZONAS
ACRE
In dispute

VENEZUELA
COLOMBIA
PERU
BOLIVIA
PARAGUAY
ARGENTINA
URUGUAY

Scale of Miles
0   200   400   600   800

N

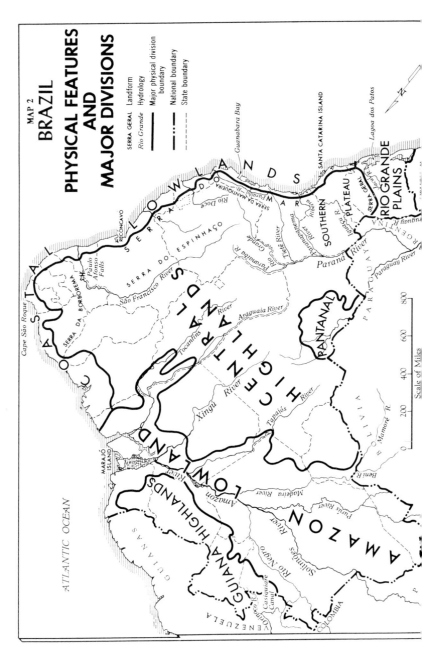

MAP 2
BRAZIL
PHYSICAL FEATURES
AND
MAJOR DIVISIONS

SERRA GERAL Landform
Rio Grande Hydrology
—— Major physical division boundary
—··—··— National boundary
- - - - - State boundary

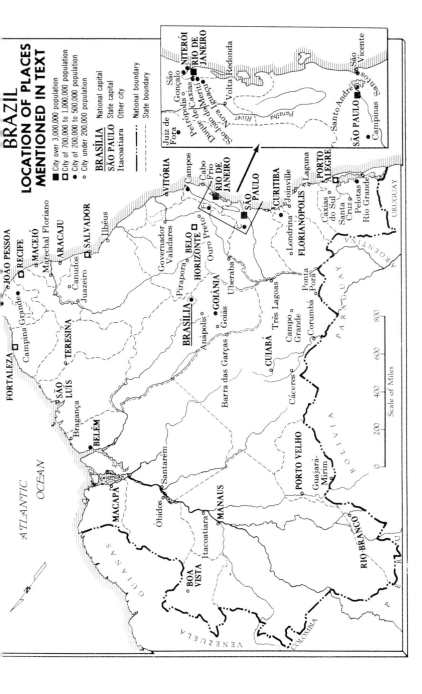

BRAZIL
LOCATION OF PLACES MENTIONED IN TEXT

■ City over 3,000,000 population
□ City of 700,000 to 1,000,000 population
○ City of 200,000 to 500,000 population
○ City under 200,000 population

BRASÍLIA   National capital
SÃO PAULO   State capital
Itacoatiara   Other city

· · · · ·   National boundary
────   State boundary

FORTALEZA
SÃO LUÍS
Bragança
BELÉM
MACAPÁ
Óbidos
Santarém
Itacoatiara
MANAUS
BOA VISTA
RIO BRANCO
PORTO VELHO
Guajará-Mirim
CUIABÁ
Cáceres
Barra das Garças
BRASÍLIA
Anápolis
GOIÁNIA
Goiás
Uberaba
Pirapora
Três Lagoas
Campo Grande
Corumbá
Ponta Porã
TERESINA
Juazeiro
Canudos
Campina Grande
JOÃO PESSOA
RECIFE
MACEIÓ
ARACAJU
Marechal Floriano
SALVADOR
Ilhéus
Governador Valadares
BELO HORIZONTE
Ouro Preto
VITÓRIA
Campos
Cabo Frio
RIO DE JANEIRO
SÃO PAULO
CURITIBA
Londrina
Joinville
FLORIANÓPOLIS
Laguna
Caxias do Sul
Santa Cruz
PORTO ALEGRE
Pelotas
Rio Grande

ATLANTIC OCEAN

GUIANAS
VENEZUELA
COLOMBIA
PERU
BOLIVIA
PARAGUAY
ARGENTINA
URUGUAY

Scale of Miles
0   200   400   600   800

Juiz de Fora
Petrópolis
São Gonçalo
NITERÓI
RIO DE JANEIRO
Duque de Caxias
Nova Iguaçu
São João de Meriti
Volta Redonda
Paraíba River
Santo André
São Paulo
SÃO PAULO
Campinas
Santos
São Vicente

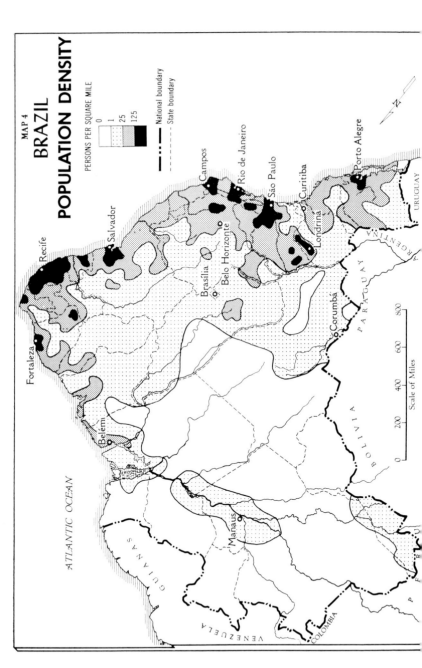

MAP 4
BRAZIL
POPULATION DENSITY

PERSONS PER SQUARE MILE

0
1
25
125

—·—·— National boundary
——— State boundary

ATLANTIC OCEAN

Fortaleza
Recife
Salvador
Belém
Brasília
Belo Horizonte
Campos
Rio de Janeiro
São Paulo
Curitiba
Londrina
Corumbá
Porto Alegre
Manaus

GUIANAS
VENEZUELA
COLOMBIA
P E R U
BOLIVIA
PARAGUAY
ARGENTINA
URUGUAY

Scale of Miles
0   200   400   600   800

N

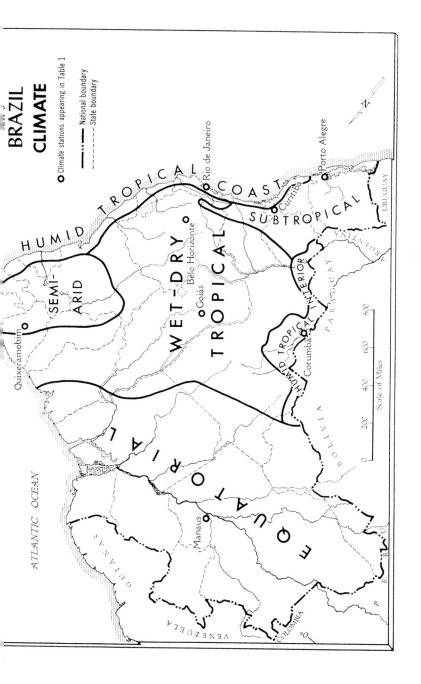

MAP 5

BRAZIL
CLIMATE

o Climate stations appearing in Table 1
--- National boundary
--·-- State boundary

ATLANTIC OCEAN

HUMID TROPICAL COAST

SEMI-ARID

Quixeramobim o

WET-DRY

Belo Horizonte
Goiás o

TROPICAL

SUBTROPICAL

Rio de Janeiro
Curitiba o
Porto Alegre o

URUGUAY

ARGENTINA

HUMID TROPICAL INTERIOR

Corumbá o

PARAGUAY

BOLIVIA

EQUATORIAL

Manaus o

GUIANAS

VENEZUELA

COLOMBIA

PERU

0°

Scale of Miles
0   200   400   600   800

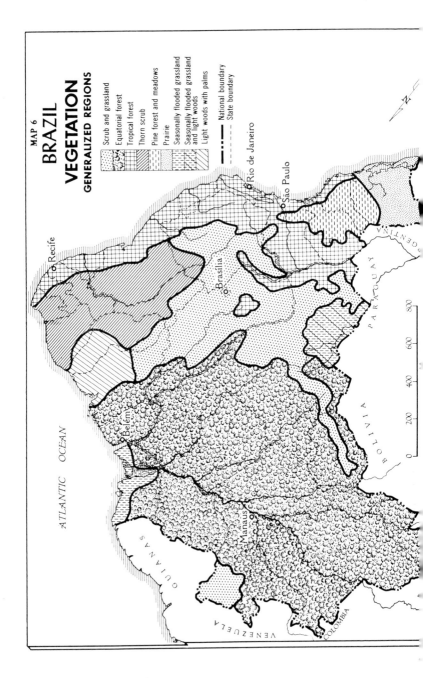

MAP 6
BRAZIL
VEGETATION
GENERALIZED REGIONS

Scrub and grassland
Equatorial forest
Tropical forest
Thorn scrub
Pine forest and meadows
Prairie
Seasonally flooded grassland
Seasonally flooded grassland and light woods
Light woods with palms

National boundary
State boundary

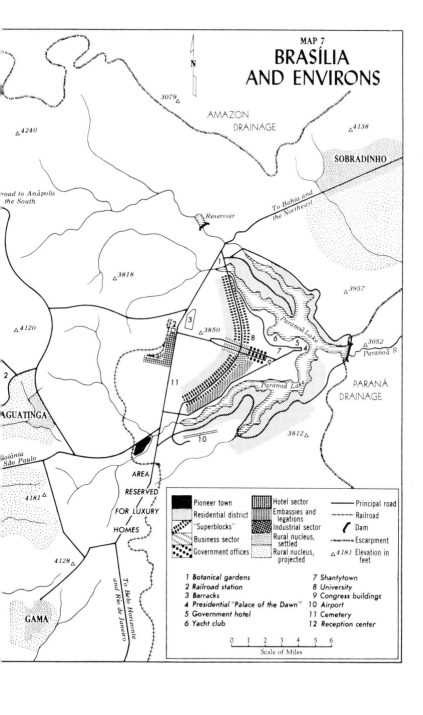

MAP 7
BRASÍLIA
AND ENVIRONS

N

AMAZON
DRAINAGE

△3079

△4240

△4138

SOBRADINHO

road to Anápolis
the South

Reservoir

To Bahia and
the Northeast

△3818

△3957

Paranoá Lake

△4120

1

2 3

△3850

8

6 5 4

△3052
Paranoá R.

2

11

9

PARANÁ
DRAINAGE

AGUATINGA

Paranoá Lake

Goiânia
São Paulo

10

3812△

△4181

AREA

RESERVED

FOR LUXURY

HOMES

△4128

GAMA

To Belo Horizonte
and Rio de Janeiro

▓ Pioneer town	▤ Hotel sector
▦ Residential district	▥ Embassies and legations
⋰ "Superblocks"	▨ Industrial sector
⋱ Business sector	⋅ Rural nucleus, settled
⋰ Government offices	⋅ Rural nucleus, projected

— Principal road
+‒+‒+ Railroad
⌐ Dam
⌇⌇⌇ Escarpment
△4181 Elevation in feet

1 Botanical gardens
2 Railroad station
3 Barracks
4 Presidential "Palace of the Dawn"
5 Government hotel
6 Yacht club

7 Shantytown
8 University
9 Congress buildings
10 Airport
11 Cemetery
12 Reception center

0   1   2   3   4   5   6
Scale of Miles

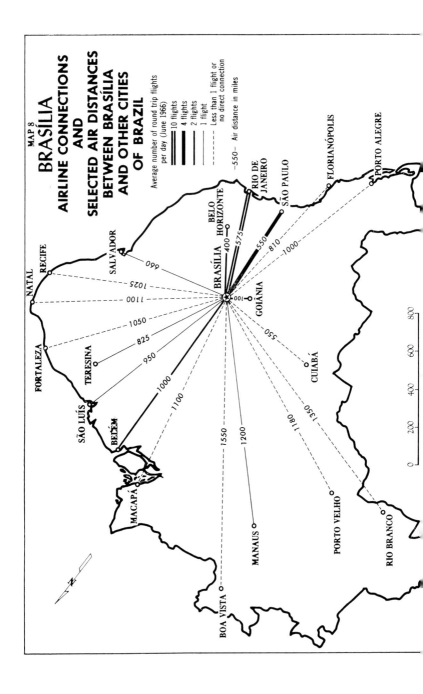

MAP 8

BRASÍLIA
AIRLINE CONNECTIONS
AND
SELECTED AIR DISTANCES
BETWEEN BRASÍLIA
AND OTHER CITIES
OF BRAZIL

Average number of round trip flights
per day (June 1966)

- 10 flights
- 4 flights
- 2 flights
- 1 flight
- Less than 1 flight or no direct connection

−550− Air distance in miles

premise that change will be the forthcoming order of the day in Brazil. This area has gained most by the nation's progress; it also has the most to lose if the country is faced with stagnation or too violent upheavals in its political, social, or economic structure. It is therefore no wonder that the people of this region have become ever more involved in the leadership of Brazil. The "Order and Progress" that is proclaimed on the flag as the national motto is fundamental to the preservation and further enrichment of a way of life which the citizens of the various states of the East have come to demand.

Brazil is a far different country in this epoch, when Marshal Castelo Branco backed by the united might of São Paulo, Minas Gerais, Rio de Janeiro, and Guanabara, routed without a shot the unstable *gaucho* President, João Goulart, than it was thirty-five years ago when another *gaucho,* Getúlio Vargas, swept into dictatorship behind his cavalry bands from Rio Grande do Sul. His reign marked the end of an era of personal, if not "personality," politics. Led by the viable and progressive East, Brazil has begun the difficult process of maturing politically, as well as economically and socially; but there are still many empty or nearly empty cars attached to the train.

5 *The Northeast*

THE Northeast, with about one-fifth of Brazil's total area, is larger than any other nation in South America except Argentina. Its population of 25 million exceeds that of every country on the continent excluding, of course, Brazil itself. Nine of Brazil's 22 states are in the Northeast; they range in size from Sergipe's 8,492 square miles (about the area of Massachusetts) to the 216,000 square miles of Bahia, which is twice as large as Ecuador, or about equal to New York and California combined. The Northeast is among the world's largest and most populous underdeveloped areas, and it is Brazil's problem region *par excellence*.

The Northeast is a classic example of underdevelopment: impoverished and ineffectively used lands; lack of opportunity compounded by the pressure of overpopulation; an uneducated and depressed peasantry; a rootless, underemployed urban proletariat; and an archaic socio-economic system under which an entrenched oligarchy is able to maintain a determined opposition to change. The consequences of such a situation are heightened by a marginal physical setting that would tax the ingenuity of a far more vigorous and imaginative system than that which orders human affairs in the Northeast.

THE SETTING

Rainfall is the most important element in the Northeast's climatic subdivisions (Map 5) and, indeed, in the entirety of its physical setting. Trending roughly northeast-southwest, there are three

74

major precipitation zones: a humid coastal strip in the east, averaging 50 to 75 miles in width, which lies across the path of the Northeast Trade Winds; a moisture-deficient middle zone that covers the larger part of the region but is most severe within the semi-arid climate area; and a zone of high rainfall in western Maranhão which is an extension of the equatorial conditions of the Amazon Basin. Naturally, there are gradations between these zones, as well as rainfall variations within them in accordance with elevation, topography, exposure to prevailing winds, and other local phenomena.

Although it is included in the Northeast for politico-statistical reasons, that part of western Maranhão which lies within the equatorial forest (Map 6) is more akin to adjoining parts of northern Goiás and eastern Pará. Much of this area has only recently been occupied by a sparse pioneering population of slash-and-burn farmers; but the somewhat denser settlement along the coast is of long standing (see Chapter 6). From an average of 80 inches a year at the edge of the equatorial forest, rainfall decreases across the zone of light woods and palms to 40 inches at its boundary with the thorn scrub. In this transition zone and along the northern coast to Cape São Roque—where rainfall values of 20 or 25 inches are mitigated by greater reliability than in the interior—very low incomes from marginal farming may be augmented by the gathering of palm nuts, from which oils are extracted. In certain districts the palm trees are grown on large plantations.

The thorn scrub, or *caatinga*, coincides approximately with that extensive part of the Northeast where rainfall averages less than 40 inches a year and may be as low as 15 inches. The extreme irregularity of precipitation here has been discussed in Chapter 1. Cattle raising is the main occupation throughout the *caatinga*, but scattered fields are cultivated in the bush, with an especial concentration near dry river beds where ground water supplies are more plentiful between periods of rain and flood. Population densities in the *caatinga*, while rather low on an absolute scale, are too high for present agro-technological conditions.

Among several districts in the *caatinga* with above-average population densities, the most important is in north-central Pernambuco, western Paraíba and Rio Grande do Norte, and southern Ceará. Here the land is higher, precipitation may reach 35 inches, and evaporation is somewhat reduced by cloud cover. Although still agriculturally marginal, especially for food crops, this is the principal cotton growing area of the Northeast. Further south, in east-central Bahia, higher population densities are found along the valleys of rivers that originate in the northern extension of the Serra do Espinhaço. Along the eastern margins of the *caatinga,* where average annual precipitation values begin to surpass 40 inches a year, a light woodland known as the *agreste* appears. The *agreste* is particularly extensive in the low mountain lands back of the coast between Salvador and Cape São Roque; and here there is a more intensive cultivation of food crops and such commercial ones as cotton, agave, sugar cane, and also coffee, since elevations attain 1,500 to 3,000 feet. These districts are also overpopulated, however, when land resources are related to current agricultural practices.

Precipitation ranges from 50 or 60 to 80 or more inches a year along the Northeast's humid tropical Trade Wind coast.[1] South of the Recôncavo heavy rainfall, a dissected topography, extensive *tabuleiros* (old terraces that form low, sandy plateaus), and poor communications limit the population to isolated communities of fishermen and subsistence farmers except where cocoa plantations have been established, particularly near Ilhéus. The Recôncavo, a plain around the bay at Salvador, is occupied by the descendants of freed slaves who evolved into smallholders specializing in tobacco but growing food crops and sugar cane as well. The more northerly coastal plains, which support some of the highest rural population

[1] It should be noted that although the winds along this coast are considered to be Trade Winds (*ventos alíseos*) and produce a climate that is characteristic of such regions, they do not conform to the classic wind zone pattern, which would have them blowing from the southeast. Rather, south of Cape São Roque the prevailing winds are from the northeast, a fact which may also help explain why there are no hurricanes in the South Atlantic Ocean.

densities in Brazil, have been growing sugar cane since colonial times—and the sugar plantation remains the foundation of their economy to this day, despite soil impoverishment, declining yields, and abysmally low living standards.

THE AGRARIAN PROBLEM

A recent report describes the lot of the tenants on a Pernambuco sugar plantation as follows: "They had to work ten hours a day, five days a week on the plantation. In return for this work they received their house, a small plot of land, and 65 cents a week, which is not necessarily paid in cash but in credit at the store operated by the administration. . . . The salary they were receiving wasn't enough to live on, so many workers had left. The plot of land they were given to produce food for home consumption . . . was about one-tenth of a hectare [one-quarter of an acre]. On this plot they planted rice, beans, and manioc [cassava]. They had two days to work their plot, [but] one of these was Sunday. If they tried to take off more time from the work required on the plantation to spend on their plot, they would be evicted. They held no rights of occupancy and could be evicted at any time. . . . Both the insecurity of occupancy and the debt relationship with the company store served as a means of enforcing the landlord's will on the workers." [2]

Elsewhere in the Northeast the tenant's relationship to the landlord follows the same general pattern, but at times under even more unstable conditions. In the cotton zone, particularly, there is a greater chance of drought than there is along the sugar growing coast. Furthermore, the cotton growers' rising demand for land and labor has, in recent years, pushed the cultivated area into drier lands even less suited for the growing of food crops and more vulnerable to droughts. Cotton production has actually worsened living conditions in the area within which it is grown. Not only are the peasants less able to grow their own food, much of which

[2] Michael Sund, "Brazilian Tenure Survey," *Land Tenure Center Newsletter,* University of Wisconsin, February 1963, pp. 6–8.

must be imported at high cost from other better watered parts of the Northeast or more distant farmlands; but a drought year will almost surely destroy both their own few subsistence crops and the cotton which provides the cash income with which food is purchased.

The peasant of the cattle raising sections of the Northeast lives in much the same manner as his counterparts in the other areas. He is also a farmer at little above the subsistence level. Roving about as a migrant tenant from ranch to ranch, he temporarily clears a small plot in the *caatinga,* growing food for his family and deriving a small cash income from any meager surplus the land may yield in years of good rainfall. He may also receive some share of any cattle he cares for on behalf of the landowner. After a few years the plot is abandoned, to be taken over by a somewhat better vegetation cover for grazing than the natural thorn scrub to which it eventually reverts. After the climax species have reinvaded the plot, it is lent out to a new tenant until it is once again improved for pasture. Living on the very margin of existence, these temporary tenants may be faced with starvation during a drought period, when dead cattle and parched crops lie dessicated under the searing sun of a land now become a desert.

In other years, floods may be as calamitous as failure of the rains, drowning cattle and sweeping away fields that have been planted near the water courses. An example of such a catastrophe was one that occurred in March, 1960, when heavy rain in its headwaters caused the Jaguaribe River of Ceará to rise 32 feet above normal. Water backed up until it stood 6 feet above the top of a 300-yard long earth dam across the river, producing a waterfall 60 feet high. The dam burst and sent 710 million cubic meters of water—four times the volume of Rio's Guanabara Bay—rushing down the valley. Few deaths were recorded because warning had been given of the impending break; but nearly a quarter of a million people had to flee the valley, in which five towns were covered by 40 feet of water. The flooded valley was soon invaded by swarms of mosquitos, so that a series of epidemics broke out; and in the neighboring communities on higher land there was no food to spare for the refugees. One group of these found itself with only 25 pounds of meat to distribute to 2,000 people! Ironically, only twenty days before the violent rains hit Ceará, crops had begun to fail for lack of rainfall, and there was not a single drop of water in the bottom of the reservoir on the Jaguaribe.

EMIGRATION, A SAFETY VALVE

Refugees, or *flagelados,* like those of the Jaguaribe Valley, frequently flee during periods of drought or flood to the coastal communities; but these are already suffering from a chronic shortage of staple foods. Scarcely able to maintain themselves, they are quite unable to effectively succor others during these emergencies. It is not uncommon, at such times, for insult to be added to injury by the merchants who stockpile scarce food supplies against a certain rise in prices. Food riots may occur—but the restraint, or resignation, of the *Nordestino,* who is seldom further than a meteorological die-cast from starvation, is far more worthy of comment under these conditions.

As might be expected the average annual per capita income of the Northeast, about US $120, is approximately one-half that for Brazil as a whole. A theoretical average family of five should have about $600 a year to spend, or less than one-third the amount available to a São Paulo household. However, while $2,000 may be reasonably representative of an average family's income in the latter state, its lesser equivalent is not very meaningful in the Northeast because of the very uneven distribution of income among the various economic groups that make up the region's population. Income is also unevenly distributed among the various political units. It ranges from a high of approximately $140 per capita in the most industrialized state, Pernambuco, to the abysmally low figure, even on a world-wide scale, of $60 in Piauí which lacks a fair share of the more productive coastland. The states of Paraíba, Sergipe, Alagoas, and Bahia fall around the $120 mark; Rio Grande do Norte, Ceará, and Maranhão have about $75 annual per capita income. These differences in levels of living are officially recognized by the Federal government through the minimum wage that is set for various parts of the country. As of February, 1965, this was highest in Guanabara State and Greater São Paulo, where the minimum wage was US $35 a month, and lowest in Piauí and Maranhão, where the figure was slightly under $20 per month. Many types of workers, including those on farms, are not covered by even these low minimum wages, which only heightens the attraction to the *Nordestino* of the economic opportunities that lie outside the region in which he was born.

Because of the lack of opportunity in the Northeast, as reflected in the low per capita income and minimum wage figures, to which must be added the possibility of natural disaster, the region, since the decline of the sugar plantation economy near the end of the seventeenth century, has supplied Brazil with much of the manpower it needed to carry out its most difficult tasks. Between 1710 and 1750 half a million *Nordestinos* migrated to the newly opened gold and diamond fields of central Minas Gerais. Between 1780 and 1820 one-quarter of a million of them moved to the coffee plantations of the Paraíba Valley in Rio, despite the competition of slavery. From 1880 to 1910 another half million migrants made possible the rubber boom in the Amazon Valley. Few of the buildings in São Paulo, Rio de Janeiro, or other cities would have been built without the labor of the *Nordestinos;* and during the past five years tens of thousands of these people have carried out the work of constructing Brasília and of settling the lands around it.

Today nearly one million people who were born in the Northeast live outside the region, providing the low-paid, unskilled workers needed to build new factories, highways, cities, and farms throughout other parts of the country. An extreme example of this out-migration can be seen in its effect on Alagoas, which has 300,-000 people working in agriculture and 33,000 in manufacturing within the state—but 150,000 employed in these occupations elsewhere in the country. Representing nearly one-third of the labor force and 16 percent of the total population, this is the highest emigration rate of any Northeastern state. Of these emigrants, 44 per-cent will some day return to Alagoas. In Bahia, on the other hand, only 8 percent of those who depart ever return. The rate of repatri-ation in the other states averages between 30 and 40 percent. Those who do return come back only after their best productive efforts have been expended elsewhere. To the benefit of other parts of Brazil, the Northeast is being drained of its best workers and most ambitious and energetic people.

THE URBAN PROBLEM

As elsewhere in the country, urbanization is proceeding at a rapid pace in the Northeast, with city populations additionally swollen from time to time by people fleeing *en masse* from the ef-fects of drought or flood. But for those fortunate few who order the destinies of the region, the cities have simply been places in which to spend lavishly the money earned from raw materials produced in the interior and sent out through their ports. Only rarely have urban areas been viewed as potential centers of production in their own right. As a result, the economic structure which has been pre-served in them is archaic, and provides little opportunity or in-centive for change. Despite this situation, in most of the Northeast about 35 percent of the population now lives in cities, with a range from 18 percent in Maranhão to 45 percent in Pernambuco.

Employment opportunities usually associated with urbanization are, however, wanting in the Northeast. In many cases the migrants have merely transferred their old way of life from the *sertão* to the cramped confines of coastal shantytowns. In some of the cities, "population groups have concentrated on swampy lands. . . . Feed-ing on shellfish picked up in shallow waters, they represent a queer form of subsistence economy on an urban basis. Their migration to the cities, rather than reflecting an occupational growth in industries and services, shows the impossibility of survival in the surrounding rural areas dominated by huge land holdings." [3]

[3] *The Brazilian Northeast,* Brazilian Embassy, Washington, D.C., August 1961, p. 12.

Salvador has a population of some 800,000, making it a very close runner-up to Porto Alegre as Brazil's fifth city; and Fortaleza has over 700,000—twice the population it had in 1960! Recife, often called the "Venice of Brazil" because of the canals left over from the days of Dutch occupation, has about one million inhabitants, which make it Brazil's third city in size. But approximately half of Recife's inhabitants live in the noisome slums which cause it to rank among the poorest of the world's large cities. The appalling conditions in these *favelas* are illustrated by the fact that, in them, infant mortality is 60 percent of births; whereas even in rural Pernambuco the figure is only 20 percent, although this is still high by world standards.

The urban proletariat has scarcely more security than the rural. It may often be in greater distress, seeking fruitlessly for a means to make a living under circumstances in which the labor force is increasing at a faster rate than new urban employment becomes available. This situation has forced the living standards of the entire lower class downward; but the city dwellers are unable to return to the marginal, unsettled existence of the rural areas, from whence catastrophe, over-population, and dissatisfaction are driving other people to swell the numbers already in the cities. Worse pressures will be avoided only by basic changes in the socio-economic structure, which is the fundamental cause of the present situation.

AN OUTMODED SOCIETY

The traditions of the Northeast go back to medieval days with its rulers and its serfs and its privileges conferred at birth rather than earned through individual initiative and ability. The cornerstone of Spanish and Portuguese colonial societies, a type of feudalism, became solidly entrenched in northeastern Brazil, where large land grants were used for sugar plantations worked by Indians and Negroes, whose low status and disfranchisement went unquestioned. The continued prevalence of the sugar (and later cotton) plantation and the ranch as a way of life has maintained this social structure to the present time. The extended family is still, essentially, the basis of power in the Northeast, and quasi-filial devotion and obedience are expected by the head of the family of his retainers, tenants, and employees. Jobs, chances for advancement, and such favors as may be bestowed—all come from the *patrão,* who, in exchange, demands absolute allegiance. The most powerful *patrões,* in turn, constitute the *coronéis,* whose rule continues to dominate the political life of the Northeast.

An underlying spirit of rebellion in the *Nordestino* is sometimes channelled into action, usually in the form of banditry but occasionally as a full-fledged, open revolt against authority. The most famous such occasion, retold in Euclydes da Cunha's "Rebellion in the Backlands" (*Os Sertões*), was the suicidal stand at Canudos of a peasant army led by the mystic Antônio Conselheiro. More recently, the Peasant Leagues organized by Francisco Julião forcefully occupied a number of plantations, some of which are now being run by small farmers as cooperatives. This movement, which at one time extended to the outskirts of Rio de Janeiro, tapered off when its leader was elected to the Chamber of Deputies and was thereby considered to have automatically joined the ranks of the oppressors. Although each episode of banditry and rebellion differs in detail, all reveal a depth of hopelessness among the Northeastern proletariat which makes it easy prey to leadership of any kind that promises a change from the status quo. Not unexpectedly, any change in the established order of things is unthinkable to the oligarchy, which uses every weapon at its command to suppress active challenges to its authority.

Under these conditions, it is not surprising that the revolutionary slogans emanating from Cuba have, in recent years, had a certain appeal to many of those who seek a new socio-economic structure for the Northeast. Unlike the self-seeking politician with whose empty slogans the *Nordestino* is all too familiar, Fidel Castro did, after all, keep his promises to the peasantry to make a genuine change. But a revolution based on Marxist ideology has not got off the ground here for a number of reasons. While the oligarchy keeps a firm grip on every aspect of the power structure, it has at the same time managed to maintain the myth that the people are living under a duly elected democracy and not under a dictatorship. The peasant movement has never been really organized, much less coordinated with that of the politically more active urban proletariat. And inspired leadership by a liberal wing within the church, headed by Archbishop Helder Câmara of Recife, has redirected much potential revolutionary energy into more acceptable channels. Finally, there is the all-important fact that the Northeast constitutes only one part of Brazil, the rest of which is either too advanced or too backward to seriously consider revolution. This larger whole also provides a positive outlet for the energies of the most dissatisfied; it has the ultimate power to crush any rebellion that may be mounted —and it has the resources whereby the Northeast may some day be liberated from its stagnation.

THE NORTHEAST—A BRAZILIAN COLONY?

Meanwhile, as a result of the inflation with which the landless rural worker and the underemployed slum dweller have been unable to cope because of their poor bargaining position, the economic plight of the *Nordestino* has intensified in recent years. Malnutrition is a chronic condition for many, and it may attain proportions of near-famine during periods of flood or drought. Diseases and malaria are endemic, and life expectancy in the Northeast is only about 30 years. Progress is hampered by widespread ignorance and illiteracy, and three-fourths of the people are not eligible to vote, disfranchised by a literacy test. Less than one-third of the children eligible for primary school are in attendance, and the average teacher in the rural areas has had only two years of primary school preparation. Of those who become wage earners, usually at the age of ten or twelve, few have more than three years of schooling.

The Northeast also suffers from an ever-worsening situation by comparison with the economically more progressive parts of the country. Table 3 illustrates this trend for the last intercensal period. The Northeast's proportion of an already inadequate share of the nation's income from industry decreased despite a slight absolute

TABLE 3

Share of National Income from Agriculture and Industry
Northeastern States as Percent of Brazilian Total

State	Agriculture 1950	1960	Industry 1950	1960	Population 1950	1960
Alagoas	1.4	1.7	0.7	0.5	2.1	1.8
Bahia	6.3	7.2	2.5	2.3	9.3	8.4
Ceará	4.0	3.4	0.9	0.7	5.2	4.7
Maranhão	1.4	2.4	0.6	0.5	3.0	3.5
Paraíba	3.1	3.4	0.6	0.4	3.3	2.8
Pernambuco	4.6	4.5	3.2	2.2	6.5	5.8
Piauí	0.8	0.8	0.2	0.1	2.0	1.8
Rio Grande do Norte	1.7	1.8	0.3	0.3	1.9	1.6
Sergipe	0.7	0.9	0.4	0.3	1.2	1.1
TOTAL NORTHEAST	24.0	26.1	9.4	7.3	34.5	31.5

increase in industrial productivity. The relative increase in the value of its agricultural production, the least remunerative for the worker, only emphasizes the reliance of that area's economy on cheap labor. Although the Northeast showed a relative decline in population compared to the country as a whole, in absolute numbers it increased from 18 to 23 million between 1950 and 1960, assuring a continued supply of workers on a depressed labor market.

As a report from the Brazilian Embassy in Washington points out, the Northeast's problems have "been aggravated in the past two decades as a result of measures taken for the industrialization of the South-Central region of Brazil." When tariff protection was granted to aid expanding national industries, the relative prices of manufactured goods increased while those of raw materials, which constituted the principal source of income for the Northeast, remained the same or in some cases even declined because of a worsening international market. Furthermore, the consistent surplus of foreign exchange earned by the Northeast, where in the late 1950's the value of exports was three times greater than that of imports, was used to a large extent for financing imports of capital and consumer goods for the benefit of the South and East. Therefore, "the contribution of the Northeast to the financing of industrialization was, relatively speaking, a very high one, even though that industrialization took place outside the region." This caused "a permanent leaching away of real income from the Northeast to the South-Central economy." [4] In this respect, the Northeast seems to bear a relationship to the East and the South similar to that of a colony to an imperialist power.

PROSPECTS FOR DEVELOPMENT

As has been the case recently throughout the world's colonial or ex-colonial areas, the demands of Brazil's underdeveloped regions on the central government have become more and more insistent. This is particularly true of the numerically powerful Northeast. First official concern for the region dates back, however, to the 1930's. At this time the National Department for Anti-Drought Works (D.N.O.C.S.) was established to deal with crises in the "Drought Polygon," which includes all of Ceará, Rio Grande do Norte, and Paraíba, most of Piauí and Pernambuco, and parts of the other states as far south as northern Minas Gerais. Under the law creating D.N.O.C.S., three percent of the Federal income tax collection was allocated to a program of public works within the Polygon. Most of the money (after considerable attrition from graft) went into roads and dams. Neither of these engineering approaches has been an unqualified success. To date, about 200 dams have been built, with a potential for irrigating nearly one quarter of a million acres; yet only 25,000 acres have actually been irrigated. The road building program operated sporadically, principally to provide employment during drought periods, and the net effect has been to retain surplus labor in the area which might otherwise have migrated to other parts of the country, thereby intensifying the food problem.

In 1945 the São Francisco Hydroelectric Company (C.H.E.S.F.) was organized, with the Brazilian government the largest share-

---

[4] *Op. cit.*, p. 3.

holder, to tap the hitherto unexploited power potential of the São Francisco River. Sometimes called the "Brazilian Nile," this 2,000-mile long river is an artery of transport from the coast to Marechal Floriano, and again between Juazeiro and Pirapora, the terminus of a railway from Minas. Between these segments the river flows at high velocity through a narrow canyon until it plunges over the 275-foot Paulo Afonso Falls (about 100 feet higher than Niagara). C.H.E.S.F. was given the concession to supply electricity to an area within a radius of 300 miles of the falls. Larger than Spain, this region included about 25 million people living within the Drought Polygon and along the Atlantic coast between Fortaleza and Salvador.

Paulo Afonso's first three generators, with a capacity of 200,000 kw, began operating in 1954, approximately doubling the consumption of electricity in the Northeast. Yet, according to the 1960 census, this still averaged only 74 kwh per capita compared to 323 kwh for Brazil as a whole. Furthermore, distribution of electricity was very uneven, with 50 and 25 percent going, respectively, to Pernambuco and Bahia, primarily for the cities of Recife and Salvador. In contrast, electricity had reached only 0.3 percent of the rural area by that date; and more than half of the C.H.E.S.F. concession was still unserved by power in 1965, when generating capacity reached 375,000 kw. Loans from the Inter-American Development Bank will, in part, aid in expanding the Paulo Afonso plant to its ultimate capacity of 915,000 kw. Some money from the same source is also being invested in a new dam, now nearing completion, on the Parnaíba River, which follows the border between Piauí and Maranhão.

In 1959 the Federal government established SUDENE, the Superintendency for the Development of the Northeast. Aimed at a more integrated approach to the development of the Northeast than had been provided by either D.N.O.C.S. or C.H.E.S.F., it was given overall authority, through centralized planning, for all aspects of regional improvement.

SUDENE's "Guiding Plans for Development," for instance, assign priorities to investments in public works so as to systematize the preceding money-wasting hodge-podge of uncoordinated projects run by separate agencies of the Federal government. This practice had frequently resulted in funds being lacking to complete works that had been started, with their subsequent deterioration. To date, SUDENE's actual accomplishments in this field include initiating eleven major highway projects and numerous ones for secondary roads, providing power to 75 rural communities and starting work toward linking up another 375, drilling or restoring about 2,000 wells to supply water for the smaller towns, and financing water supply and sewage projects in 125 cities.

SUDENE also has, as one of its principal objectives, the general up-grading of the socio-economic milieu of the Northeast, to be achieved primarily through education. At present the organization is helping to pay for the construction of classrooms (750 were built in 1965 alone), providing teacher training (2,500 were involved in 1965), and aiding various programs in adult and technical education. It has established 500 scholarships for advanced training in engineering, agronomy, and animal husbandry. Such programs are essential for the long-range improvement of the human environment of this region, but their effects will be slow and diffuse. The question remains whether SUDENE or any other official organization will have the incentive and the courage to institute an even more necessary reorganization of the existing social and economic order. Or will the program lose its impetus once the most glaring injustices are erased or hidden behind a façade of show-piece projects? The future political stability of the Northeast depends upon the answer to these questions.

More tangible, perhaps, are SUDENE's ambitious schemes for achieving the economic development of the Northeast through "Five Year"-type plans, which coordinate government projects with incentives to private enterprise. Its objectives were laid down in the first of such plans, which was prepared in 1961 after a series of delays created by conservative elements in Congress. These objectives were 1) increasing industrial investment; 2) augmenting the production of sugar cane and food crops by more intensive use of the humid coastal zone; 3) expanding agriculture in the Drought Polygon by achieving better ecological equilibrium; and 4) intensifying settlement of the agricultural frontiers in the humid lands of southern Bahia and western Maranhão.

Among the three agricultural objectives stated in the 1961 plan, the last will be the most readily attainable. Rural nuclei, using experience gained in planned farming settlements in the West and South, have already been established in the Maranhão forests, where spontaneous colonization has also taken place along recently built roads. Elsewhere, in the long occupied and relatively densely populated rural areas of the Northeast, it will be exceedingly difficult to bring about improvements in traditional farming methods and institutions. The natural inertia of any such outmoded rural system will certainly be reinforced by the long-standing aversion of the landowners to investing in the modernization of their establishments, particularly since their individual needs are adequately provided for under current practices. Furthermore, SUDENE's resources for this monumental undertaking are limited at present, and only 12.9 percent of the budget of the Three-Year Plan that began in 1966 is earmarked for "agriculture and marketing," compared to 49 percent for public works or 13.4 percent for manpower training.

Other sectors for which funds were allocated under the Three-Year Plan include a 6 percent share for SUDENE's administrative expenses, 7.4 percent for natural resources development, and 5.8 percent for "special programs" such as the one in which a mission of 20 French technicians is studying the water problems of the Jaguaribe Valley. Finally, 5.5 percent of SUDENE's resources during 1966–1968 has been spent on research and incentives for industry. The approximately US $40 million which this represents (out of a total budget of $250 million a year for the three year period) is, as it were, only the tip of the iceberg, as SUDENE expects to have attracted a further $600 million in private investments to the Northeast in those years.

The key to SUDENE's program for stimulating private industrial investment is its approval of projects, which thereby become entitled to various advantages such as the right to apply for government loans, exemption from import duties on equipment, Federal income tax reductions, and the opportunity for a corporation to use half of its tax liabilities incurred elsewhere in the country for investment in the Northeast. Most of the Northeastern states are now themselves contributing to this approach for attracting industry, with additional loans and tax exemptions as well as assistance in acquiring building sites. It is interesting to note that Pernambuco, which presently accounts for one-third of all industrial production in the Northeast, began such a program in 1952 in conjunction with building an industrial park at Cabo, 25 miles from Recife, and organizing a state shipping company to facilitate transport. In mid-1967 Salvador also organized an industrial park nearby, at Aratu, almost immediately attracting 32 companies to sign building contracts for investments totaling US $70 million, the principal manufactures being chemicals, plastics, cement products, and foodstuffs.

As a result of these measures, the Northeast is now receiving between 15 and 20 percent of Brazil's private investment, compared to only 3 percent in 1960. Even in official Federal undertakings prior to 1961, the Northeast received short shrift in comparison with the more developed parts of the country. This is demonstrated by the fact Brazil's National *Development* Bank (italics are the author's), during the first ten years of its operation, allocated 92.3 percent of its assistance for private industry to companies located in the south-central part of the country; whereas only 4.4 percent of such funds went to the Northeast. In an attempt to remedy this situation, SUDENE established the Investment Fund for the Economic and Social Development of the Northeast, which is financed through the Federal tax reduction framework. In 1962 the Fund yielded some US $6 million for investment in the Northeast, and by 1965 the figure had risen to nearly $70 million. As a result of these various measures, the number of SUDENE-approved private investment projects in the Northeast increased from 23 plants during its first year of operation to 103 new industries in 1965.

The products of industrial plants recently attracted to the Northeast range from radios to refrigerators, from nylon yarn to tires, and from oil drills to a wide array of items used by the building trades. A $33 million synthetic rubber plant, using by-product alcohol from the sugar industry, will cut Brazil's imports of this substance in half. A plant to assemble Jeeps is also being built. This last may be used to illustrate the current economic relationship of the Northeast vis-a-vis the East: before the Willys company began manufacturing Jeeps in Brazil, American-made ones were assembled near Rio de Janeiro; now that the center of gravity of industrial development has shifted so that the primary production of vehicles is within Brazil itself, assembly is taking place in an underdeveloped region inside the national boundaries. Another example of this internal neo-colonialism is a steel mill SUDENE is building in Bahia. As the U.S. once helped build the East's Volta Redonda plant, now money originating in the East will be used for one in the Northeast. On the other hand, the East is being by-passed by a number of U.S. firms which have been attracted by the new investment incentives—even to the extent of setting up an aeroplane industry in the Northeast, where a few years ago American interests were confined to palm oil plantations and a few mining enterprises.

The question remains whether SUDENE will be able in the long run to attract capital and know-how to the Northeast in sufficient quantity and of high enough quality to trigger the development it is hoping for, or whether the majority of current investments will merely satisfy the classic demands of a neo-colonial society for greater economic self-sufficiency. This will be the key to the future economic development of the region. SUDENE has made a reasonable beginning, but despite the examples cited of rather spectacular types of industries recently attracted to the Northeast, most of the new ones have, in fact, been basic processors of locally produced raw materials taking advantage of artificial incentives, cheap labor, and an unsatisfied market formerly supplied from the East and the South. The road toward economic betterment that lies ahead of the Northeast will be a long and difficult one, especially as the major highways of industrial and agricultural progress still lead to the East.

The central government must continue to play a leading role in up-grading the Northeast's economy as, if it does not, the *Nordestinos* will have to resign themselves to the role of an underdeveloped area supplying cheap manpower and low value raw materials to the wealthier and ever more prosperous parts of the country. Under such conditions the area will continue to find itself unable to solve its most basic socio-economic problems. But until they are solved, the *Nordestino* will in ever increasing numbers continue to be the victim of feudal-minded landlords, avaricious storekeepers, and unscrupulous politicians, whose grip on the region is made more unbearable by the twin catastrophes of flood and drought.

6   *The North*

T HE Amazon, mightiest of the world's rivers, gives the North of Brazil its distinctive character. As yet uncounted tributaries, fifteen of them over one thousand miles long, constitute the vast hydrographic network of the Amazon Basin, which drains an area as large as the United States and within which is the most extensive equatorial forest on earth. The Amazon River, which contributes one-fifth of all the fresh water that flows into the oceans, is the most eminently navigable of all the world's river systems; yet it is little used by twentieth-century man, and no bridge spans the river throughout its entire 4,000-mile course. Even its history is uncertain. Although the official discovery of Brazil is credited to Cabral in 1500 (Chapter 2), there is strong if indirect evidence to support the notion that the Amazon delta had been discovered before 1498. From December of that year to May of 1499, an expedition under a Portuguese captain Maranhão is believed to have explored upriver for 500 miles, to the mouth of the Tapajós.

Fifty-six percent of Brazil's territory is located within the Amazon drainage basin, as are large sections of other South American countries that face the Pacific. The Brazilian North, or "Amazonia" as it is sometimes called, has however, traditionally been limited to those states and territories which are oriented toward and dependent upon communications along the river: Pará, Amazonas, Amapá, Roraima (formerly Rio Branco), Acre, and Rondônia (formerly Guaporé). Forty-two percent of Brazil's area is accounted for by these six political units, with exactly one-third of the country falling within the boundaries of two states, Amazonas and Pará. The former has 18 percent of the national territory, covering 600,000 square miles; Pará, with about 480,000 square miles, includes 15 percent of Brazil. Alaska is a bit smaller than Amazonas and slightly larger than Pará.

Those enormous states dwarf by comparison the newly-created Acre State, previously a territory, which has an area of 57,900 square miles, and the territories of Rondônia (92,640 square miles), Roraima (88,780 square miles), and Amapá (54,040 square miles). Yet the smallest of these is larger than Pennsylvania, in the United States, or than nine Brazilian states, including five of those in the Northeast, Espírito Santo, Rio de Janeiro, Santa Catarina, and of course Guanabara.

Similar superlatives cannot, however, be said to apply in the matter of demography. Within the North's nearly 1½ million square miles live under three million people, constituting less than 4 percent of the Brazilian total. The overall population density is only 2 per square mile, about the same as Greenland or the Sahara. Furthermore, these people are very unevenly distributed, being concentrated in the major cities and towns or scattered in small communities along the more accessible waterways. About 1.8 million people, or approximately half the total population of the North, are located in Pará—and nearly one-third of these are in Belém. A large proportion of the rest of Pará's inhabitants live within a strip of land between the capital and Bragança, along a recently discontinued railroad. Compared to Belém's population of 500,000 the emptiness of Amazonas is striking, the entire state having only some 800,000 people (fewer than in any other Brazilian state except Acre and Sergipe), nearly one quarter of whom live in Manaus.

This demographic dominance by the capitals increases with the decreasing size of the smaller political units, within which they represent practically the only places with even minimal amenities and opportunities. Thus, Acre has about 180,000 inhabitants, of which 60,000, or one-third of the total, live in Rio Branco City. The 65,000 people in Porto Velho represent more than two-thirds of

Rondônia's population of 90,000. Amapá has about the same total number of inhabitants as Rondônia, but nearly three-fourths of these are in Macapá. Almost the entire population—30,000 out of 35,000—of Roraima Territory is in Boa Vista.

This extreme nucleation of Amazonian settlement exists within the demographic void of the surrounding tropical rain forest. The imbalance of urban to rural population ratios seems anomalous, given the degree of underpopulation and underdevelopment which exists in the North, where the economic support of those who inhabit the settlements must come almost entirely from the gathering of forest products and the crops of the few minute clearings beside nearby waterways. Only in Pará is a statistically significant amount of land devoted to agriculture and urban use, and this amounts to less that 1.5 percent of the state's total area. It almost seems as though the people of the North are clinging together, as the first settlers must have done in the coastal jungles of Brazil 400 years ago, for protection against the forces of nature which are poised on their doorstep, ready to overwhelm the fragile settlements at the slightest sign of inattention. This vast and seemingly remote region can only be comprehended in terms of its physical setting, the basis for human activity in the North.

THE LAND AND THE WATER

The North includes an often not appreciated variety of landform and vegetation characteristics which are, in turn, of fundamental importance to soil and land use patterns. Some of these features appear on Maps 3 and 6, but others occur on so small a scale as to be capable of depiction on only the most detailed maps. The brief paragraphs that follow will outline the most important of these physical units.

The formations of the Guiana and Central Highlands in the northern and southern headwaters of the Amazon Basin are dissected into tablelands, ridges, and hills as they approach the main valley. Low outliers of these, known as the *terra-firme,* occasionally border the river where, as at Santarém and Manaus, they make ideal settlement sites because they lie above the highest flood level. On the other hand, the *terra-firme* is an old landform the soils of which have been thoroughly leached and impoverished, so that it is among the worst areas for agriculture. The highest parts may be scrub-covered and therefore suited only for grazing.

The Amazon Lowlands are made up of deposits of river alluvium of various ages, built up to form a sedimentary basin. In the west this plain extends 900 miles from north to south, but downstream from Manaus it is much narrower, pinched in between the river and outliers of the *terra-firme*. Below the Xingú the floodplain broadens out again, and in the Amazon Estuary delta deposits form innumerable islands, the largest of which, Marajó, is about the size of Switzerland. Subsidence of the lower reaches of the main stream, where the alluvium is many thousands of feet thick, has entrenched its lesser tributaries, creating falls and rapids along them. In the broad western part of the basin this process has left considerable portions of older sediments in the interfluves free from flooding, so that they may be considered a recent variety of the *terra-firme*, with soils that are also leached and therefore infertile under their cover of equatorial forest.

That portion of the floodplain which is covered to various depths by the waters of the annual floods is known as the *várzea*. The waterways meander over this part of the plain, shifting their courses and producing a characteristic pattern of natural levees, abandoned channels, oxbow lakes, swamps, under-cut banks, and slipoff slopes. Some *várzea* lands are wet almost all of the time; other parts may be flooded for only brief periods; and the so-called "high" *várzea* is flooded only in exceptional years. The last may be fairly extensive, but most commonly it consists of discontinuous ridges, the remnants of old levees.

The high *várzea*, which is always forested in its native state, is the preferred location for villages and individual huts because the threat of being flooded out is minimized. As a matter of convenience it is therefore the high *várzea* that is the most frequently cultivated. However, as these are the oldest of the *várzea* lands, and therefore the most leached, and as they are only rarely renewed by fresh silt deposition, they are less fertile than most of the lands of the annually flooded "low" *várzea*.

The lands of the low *várzea* frequently consist of natural levees in the process of formation, covered every year by normal flood waters. The soils are therefore younger than those of the high *várzea,* their nutrients renewed by fresh deposits of river silt. These lower levees are, like the older and higher ones, tree covered, but the forest tends to be less dense and more homogeneous. These are among the best agricultural lands of the Amazon Basin, but the difficulty of establishing permanent habitations upon them has caused them to be neglected unless they are located within reach of higher and drier lands. Planting is done soon after the waters recede, and the crops are harvested before flooding covers the land again.

One of several special types of low *várzea* is found on slipoff slopes around the bends of the larger rivers. These slipoff slopes are made up entirely by deposits of fresh silt and are therefore very fertile, with the additional advantage of being devoid of vegetation. Well drained and easy to plant, they are seeded at low water, sometimes very intensively with a cash crop such as rice or beans, by people who live on higher ground and may travel to their "farms" by canoe. At the other extreme, the low *várzea* also includes large areas of poorly drained, clayey lands, where water remains standing for much of the year. Found in the bottoms of oxbows and abandoned channels, or on land that is so flat the floodwaters will not flow off, they are too wet for farming or even for forest growth. Grass-covered, this waterlogged *várzea* is often used for cattle grazing if it is sufficiently extensive, the largest herds being on Marajó Island. To keep the animals from drowning at flood time they may be driven to higher ground or even placed on rafts which float for months half-submerged in water. As the cattle must, under the best of circumstances, spend much of their time wading in the water, their hooves and legs are frequently harmed.

It can be appreciated that the North has a considerable variety of land types, each with well defined characteristics that are understood by the natives who are attuned to the nuances of this tropical riverine environment. From an agronomist's point of view, two characteristics stand out: first, well drained areas with soils that are renewed annually are able to produce continuously high yields of a great variety of crops; and second, such lands are difficult to organize because they are scattered almost randomly throughout the length and breadth of the river basin. In their totality these low *várzea* silts, despite the fact that they comprise only about 1.5 percent of the Amazon Basin, amount to over 50,000 square miles, an area greater than that of Rio de Janeiro and Espírito Santo States combined. Yet these last two mountainous and underutilized states, with their difficult and expensive transportation problems, support over five million inhabitants, roughly twice as many as the entire North. It is, therefore, not simply a lack of resources which accounts for the demographic vacuum and low standard of living that presently characterize "Amazonia"; many of its problems are at least partly cultural in origin.

THE COURSE OF SETTLEMENT

Although Europeans have lived amidst, and exploited, the resources of the North for hundreds of years and the native Indians have done so for thousands, its vastness remains virtually unchanged by the hand of man, and many of the opportunities it offers are still little known and even less appreciated. To fully understand the neglect of this area which borders the greatest of all tropical rivers and is closer and more easily accessible to the markets of Europe and temperate North America than are India, Java, or even the coastal lowlands of more southerly Brazil, one must understand the background and the nature of the exploitation of both its lands and its people.

The center *par excellence* of the Indian culture described in Chapter 1 was, and in certain remote headwaters still is, in the Amazon Basin. This culture was scarcely disturbed during the first two and a half centuries of European incursions into the New

World. It is true that in 1615 a Portuguese settlement was established at Belém by people sent to the Amazon from São Luís do Maranhão to prevent the English and Dutch from occupying this part of Portuguese territory; but few Europeans were involved and their activities were very limited.

It was the ubiquitous Jesuits who, after establishing a mission at Belém in 1616, extended the occupation of the Amazon further upstream. Unlike the settlers of Maranhão and those along the coast to the south, where plantations were organized on the basis of slave labor, the Jesuits left the Indians in their villages, organizing and catechizing them and getting them to extract exportable items from the forest and to grow the tropical crops for which there was a market in Europe. In exchange, the Indians received manufactured goods and protection against the slave-raiding *Maranhaenses*. So successful were the Jesuits that Pará was allowed to function as an isolated, self-governing nucleus within the Portuguese colonial system. By the middle of the eighteenth century the missions were exporting significant quantities of cocoa, vanilla, cinnamon, cloves, indigo, aromatic resins, and cabinet woods; but exact quantities cannot be determined as the Jesuits paid no taxes and kept no books.

The Jesuit hegemony in the Amazon was shattered in 1759 when the Order was banished from the Portuguese Kingdom by the Marquis of Pombal. Their departure was followed by a wave of enslavement, Indian numbers being further reduced by epidemics of smallpox, measles, and other diseases brought in by the Europeans. Whereas the Indians in the Jesuit missions alone had totaled over 100,000, it has been estimated that by 1825 the entire population of the Brazilian Amazon was less than 40,000, despite the fact that during the second half of the eighteenth century, farming had been established at the mouth of the Amazon, principally in the vicinity of Belém. Tropical crops such as sugar cane, rice, cotton, and coffee were grown there on plantations that were integrated into the more advanced economy of Maranhão, under the auspices of a trading company that had been founded during Pombal's administration. To carry out these activities, some 30,000 African slaves had been brought to the Amazon by the end of the eighteenth century to bolster the recalcitrant Indian labor force, but a high proportion of them died from mistreatment and disease. In the long run, commercial export agriculture at the mouth of the river was unable to compete with the more efficient plantations in other parts of the country, and the region reverted to a primitive economy based upon shifting cultivation on scattered plots and haphazard gathering of forest products, only a few small plantations of coffee, cacao, tobacco, and citrus fruits remaining around some of the river-bank settlements by the middle of the nineteenth century.

THE RUBBER BOOM

Among the raw materials that were gathered from the Amazonian forest, rubber began to be exported in small quantities during the first quarter of the nineteenth century after limited commercial uses had been found for it. Following Goodyear's discovery of vulcanization in 1839, the demand increased substantially. Brazil's rubber exports, which were less than 50 tons a year in the 1820's, reached an average of 460 tons during the 1840's, nearly 2,000 tons per annum in the 1850's, and twice that during the 1860's. Within this period the price of rubber went up from £45 to £180 a ton, and the rubber boom was in full swing. Just before World War I, when the price of rubber surpassed £500 a ton, the Amazon was exporting 35,000 tons a year.

But in 1876 an English botanist, who was supposedly on a scientific expedition to the Amazon, returned to Kew Gardens with 70,000 seeds of the rubber tree, *Heavea brasiliensis,* in his valise. From these the British established rubber plantations in the East Indies. In 1914 production from southeastern Asia surpassed that of Brazil and continued to expand in organized fashion, as the wild rubber gatherers in the equatorial forests of the North were never able to do. Those distant plantations were not only able to satisfy a world-wide demand which reached hundreds of thousands of tons by the 1920's, but to bring the price down to a fraction of what it had formerly been, thereby once more reducing the value of the rubber collected in the Amazon to a level scarceley higher than that of the various other forest products. The boom, therefore, collapsed.

At the beginning of the rubber boom there were, as has been noted, only a few tens of thousands of inhabitants available to gather the latex from the rubber trees that were widely spaced through the Amazon forest. More manpower was needed, but slavery, which was already on the wane in Brazil, would have proven impracticable since the task required a multitude of individuals scattered thinly through the jungle. Fortuitously, the need coincided with a series of calamitous droughts in the overcrowded Northeast, leaving stricken people open to blandishments concerning a new life that awaited them in the Amazon. They could scarcely conceive of an existence worse than the one in which they found themselves. It has been estimated that more than a half million *Nordestinos* were induced to move to the North during the rubber boom, causing the population to increase to 330,000 by 1872, to 700,000 by 1900, and to 900,000 by 1910. Every increase in population was reflected in a rise in production of that ever more valuable commodity, rubber.

Extraction was organized and controlled by entrepreneurs who purchased the rights to vast tracts of land along the waterways, access to which could be controlled from a trading post located downstream. Agents in Belém and Manaus recruited the workers, who were then set down at intervals along the river banks, where they built their huts and cut their paths through the forest to as many rubber trees as could be reached in a day's walk. They began life as *seringueiros* in debt for their passage, their rubber-gathering equipment, and even for the canned foods on which they would live, since rubber collecting would leave them neither the time nor the energy to grow their own food. The number and density of the rubber trees, upon which their ability to make a living or even to stay alive depended, was a matter of pure chance.

The entrepreneur's launch would ply its appointed rounds, picking up the balls of latex which the *seringueiros* coagulated over their open fires. The *seringueiro* had no control over the price he received, and payment was in the form of credit against his debt and of advances against future purchases of equipment and food, bought at the entrepreneur's store at his own inflated prices. The migrants were soon inextricably bound by a debt which only in exceptional cases could ever be paid off. Those who tried to escape were either picked up immediately while trying to pass the downstream station or were returned by the authorities in whatever town or city they reached, for non-payment of debts. Few ever returned to the Northeast to tell the real story, and as the ranks of earlier migrants were thinned by accident, malnutrition, and disease, their places were taken by others who were talked into seeking a better life in the North.

The better life did exist—for some—as, thanks to the toil of the hapless *seringueiro,* wealth flowed into the Amazon on a scale unprecedented in any of the other of Brazil's booms. It filled the pockets of the entrepreneurs, the traders, the landowners, and the businessmen of Óbidos, Santarém, Belém, and especially Manaus. In the heart of the Amazon Basin, nearly 1,000 miles from the sea and surrounded by forest, Manaus became one of the earliest cities in Brazil to install electric lighting and a streetcar system. It built a floating dock, which is still in use today, so that ocean-going steamers could unload their cargoes and take aboard the precious rubber regardless of the flood stage of the river, which sometimes exceeds 50 feet. An opera house was also built at Manaus, with plush seats, gilt ornaments, lavish murals, and a huge mosaic dome inlaid with the pattern of the Brazilian flag. Passenger ships from Europe and America brought in some of the world's greatest entertainers, who braved yellow fever and other epidemics to obtain their share of the wealth which flowed into this equatorial outpost of civilization.

Before the rubber boom collapsed, one final monument was built to it—the Madeira-Mamoré Railroad. It was second only to the Panama Canal in hardships endured and lives lost during the white man's conquest of the American tropics. Like the canal, it was started once (in 1878) and abandoned because of the high death toll; but interest revived when Brazil wrested Acre (a major area of rubber production which today still accounts for 40 percent of the nation's latex) from Bolivia in 1903. The final settlement included a pledge from Brazil to resume building the railroad from the head of navigation on the Madeira at Porto Velho (see Maps 2 and 3), around the falls blocking that river, and, bridging the Mamoré, over to the navigable portion of the Beni in northeastern Bolivia. At the cost, it is said, of a workman dead for every tie laid, the railroad reached Guajará-Mirim on the Brazilian side of the Madeira; but there it halted forever in 1913.

The Madeira-Mamoré Railroad was only one of many projects dreamed up in those heady days. Others involved not only more railroads, but also a series of canals which were to link the Amazon with the Orinoco and Paraguay Rivers and turn it into a "South American Rhine." Perhaps the technological and economic capacities of the time would have been inadequate to carry out these enormous tasks; in any case, with the collapse of the rubber boom, they never left the drawing boards.

A scattering of *seringueiros'* huts and a few somnolent towns were soon all that remained of that era of superficial splendor, as the North reverted to a stagnation from which it is only beginning, fitfully, to emerge. Whether a more enlightened policy of investing the profits from rubber in the land on which it grew and in the education and health of the people who collected it would have greatly altered the course of economic events, is a matter for speculation. But the exploitative attitudes of the boom certainly produced little in the way of real progress, and they still infect the thinking of many of those who control the North's present destinies.

PROSPECTS FOR CHANGE

Today, life in most of the North remains much the same as it has been in the past. The majority of its working people are still dependent upon agriculture, much of it at the subsistence level, and the collection of forest products for a livelihood. It is not surprising that, between them, Pará and Amazonas States account for only 2.2 percent of the national income, although they include 3.2 percent of Brazil's population. The inhabitants of Amazonia, unevenly dispersed along the main waterways (Map 4), are unhealthy, poor, and uneducated, and live at such a low technological level that they can take only incomplete advantage of whatever opportunities the environment may offer.

Two crops, jute and black pepper, were introduced during the past couple of decades by Japanese immigrants, and have been important factors in reorienting thinking about the agricultural potential of the North, particularly as the production of each already exceeds that of rubber in value. Ironically, black pepper seeds reached the Amazon after being smuggled out of Singapore, thereby, as a Manaus exporter put it, "avenging the perfidy of Britain's *Heavea* seed theft." Planted on the *terra-firme* near Belém and Manaus, pepper grows most successfully when intensively fertilized. For this purpose the Japanese often raise chickens, thereby further benefitting from the sale of eggs and poultry in the cities to add to their income, which is already well above the average for the region. Black pepper production amounted to 350 tons when it first appeared among Brazil's agricultural statistics in 1952. Today the figure is over 6,000 tons a year (85 percent of it from Pará), one half of which is exported, and Brazil now ranks fifth among the world's producers of black pepper, with excellent prospects for expansion.

Jute, which is grown on the low *várzea,* was not noted statistically until after 1945. By 1954 production had reached 23,000 tons; and today it amounts to some 65,000 tons. About one-quarter of the jute comes from Pará, and three-quarters from Amazonas. Whereas less than 20 years ago Brazil's needs for this product were met by imports from the Ganges delta, including even the bags for its coffee, these are now satisfied from local plants along the Amazon, with a surplus of several thousand tons of raw and processed jute available for export each year.

The Japanese impact along the Amazon, particularly in the low *várzea,* does not stop at those two products, however. They have shown, for the first time, that it is advantageous to plant pasture grasses there, using varieties they brought with them, on which they now graze water buffalo from Indochina and cattle from Pakistan. Their vegetable gardens supply towns and cities and demonstrate that a variety of high-quality produce can be grown in the region with a little care. Introducing techniques learned in Formosa, the Japanese have also been irrigating plantations of rice and are obtaining much higher yields than under the prevailing system of growing it on dry lands after the flooding has receded. Although the Japanese today (1968) constitute only about 0.2 percent of the North's total population, they have already had an impact on its economy out of all proportion to their numbers. It will be a long time before their hard work and technological abilities are equaled by the descendents of the *seringueiros,* but some emulation is starting to take place, attested to by the scraggly, unfertilized black pepper bushes and the unkempt jute fields of the native farmer.

The gathering of forest products, as well as such related activities as hunting and fishing, is still carried out in the traditional, not to say primitive, manner. The same applies to most lumbering operations, despite the fact that the forests of the North, accessible by means of thousands of miles of navigable waterways, constitute the world's greatest potential source of hardwoods. Although 97 species with a wide diversity of physical and mechanical properties are listed in the catalogs of some 100 sawmills in the region, less than 2 percent of Brazil's timber and lumber production comes from the North. Pará provides 1.2 percent, while Amazonas accounts for a mere 0.5 percent, and production in Acre and the territories is insignificant.

In part, the very diversity of tree types is a handicap, as not all the species are in equal demand. Selective cutting, using axes to fell the trees and cut them to log length, manhandling them to the stream banks on rollers, and distributing them through many small middlemen—it is an expensive undertaking yielding very little income. Mechanization, the opening of logging roads, and a reorganization of milling and selling practices—steps similar to those which have been taken in the Rio Doce Valley and in parts of Africa—are needed to put the industry on its feet. A hopeful sign for the future is the recent establishment of two plants, one belonging to a Dutch company in Amapá and the other to a São Paulo firm at Manaus, to produce a total of about 4,000 cubic feet of plywood and veneer a month. If these are successful, others will certainly follow. Also, experiments made in São Paulo which demonstrated that hardwoods could be used in the manufacture of pulp and paper should be a stimulus to fuller utilization of the North's great forest resources.

The subsoil resources of the North are even less known than those on the surface, although airborne magnetometer and other surveys have recently been undertaken to obtain fuller information. The mineralized formations are either buried under thousands of feet of sediment or outcrop in remote and inaccessible headwater areas. Gold and diamonds have been placer mined for centuries along the outer rim of the region in the Central and Guiana Highlands, and a few minor oil wells are producing in Peru on the shallow fringes of the sedimentary basin from formations that are presumed also to extend beneath the Amazon Lowland at great depths. In Amapá, however, the Amazon Estuary approaches an outlier of the Guiana Highlands in which deposits of iron ore, chromite, cobalt, and nickel are found, and where cassiterite has been mined for a number of years in small but sufficient quantities to supply a recently built tin extracting plant at Macapá.

The most important mineralogical event ever to take place in the North has been the development of Amapá's Serra do Navio manganese deposit, South America's largest, with at least 25 million tons of 50 percent ore. It was only discovered in 1946, but in 1957 the first cargo of manganese ore left Amapá. By then, a 122-mile railroad had been built between the mine and Macapá, docks had been constructed for that port, and a channel had been dredged to handle ocean-going ships. Up to January 1965, nearly 6 million tons of ore had been shipped to Brazilian factories and to the Bethlehem mills in the United States. Serra do Navio manganese now accounts for about 3 percent of the value of Brazil's exports.

The impact this development has had on the hitherto neglected territory of Amapá has been great. In 1940 Amapá had one tiny 5 kw thermal-electric station; whereas by 1955 there were half a dozen plants with a capacity of 200 kw; and in 1961 Amapá's 7,000 kw capacity exceeded that of the entire state of Amazonas (today's figures are the same for Amapá, 25,000 kw for Amazonas, and 40,000 for Pará, while the combined capacity of the three lesser political units is about two-thirds that of Amapá). Meanwhile, during the 1950–1960 intercensal period the population of Macapá Township increased from 21,000 to 47,000, and now stands at 70,000, attracted there not only by the bright new lights of the town, but also by new schools, hospitals, roads, and above all, opportunities for employment. Such modern style "exploiting" of Amazonian resources is producing far different results from those of the rubber boom days. This change is emphasized by the fact that the largest Brazilian stockholder in the Serra do Navio mining company has used some of his profits to establish, in a hitherto undreamt of act of altruism, a private foundation for research into education, regional development, and agriculture, with an experiment station already starting to carry out the last.

That provincialism and archaic attitudes have not disappeared from the North, however, was farcically demonstrated in May of 1965, when a team of foresters and agriculturalists from the U.S. National Academy of Sciences outlined a program to the Brazilian Minister of Agriculture for establishing a tropical research and training center for Anglo and Latin Americans in Pará. Despite the fact that it was not even to be in his state and that proposals for two other centers, in Pernambuco and Peru, went virtually unnoticed, Amazonas' Governor Artur Reis attacked the plan, claiming that the Americans were trying to "internationalize" the Amazon. The press gave the statement wide coverage, and soon various important people, including the Congressmen from Amazonas, the Governor of São Paulo, and even the Minister of Planning, were issuing public pronouncements against such "internationalization." The, as one Rio paper put it, "small tempest in a huge teapot" finally brought President Castelo Branco to Belém for a major policy speech. He said that the Federal government would certainly not permit foreign powers to control the Amazon, but that it was high time this part of the country was developed and the standard of living of its people raised—and that if foreign cooperation were needed for this, the government would not allow "false nationalism" to prevent bringing the benefits of such cooperation, already extended to other parts of the country, to the North.

The task of development will certainly not be an easy one, since it must confront the extreme poverty of the backwoodsman, a rudimentary general technological level, and a serious shortage of capital, as well as a "pre-capitalist system of personal relations upon which the mechanism of production and circulation of wealth" is based.[1] The Brazilian Constitution of 1946 included an article which stipulated that for a period of at least 20 years 3 percent of the national tax revenue was to be devoted to the economic development of the Amazon. Since 1953 the program has been under the direction of a Federal agency, S.P.V.E.A. (Superintendency of the Plan for the Economic Valorization of the Amazon), the major objectives of which have been stated as 1) securing fuller occupancy of the basin, 2) improving the economy of the region, and 3) integrating the North more fully into the Brazilian economy.

S.P.V.E.A. has focused its attention on public works in 28 areas within the North, selected for their improvement potential, in order to try to get the greatest effectiveness out of the limited funds available. In 1962 tax exemptions were granted for from 5 to 20 years to companies in the Amazon processing local raw materials, in the hope of attracting private investments. Yet loans to private industry by Brazil's National Development Bank gave the North a share that amounted only to an insignificant 0.7 percent of the total! In

[1] Afrânio Melo, "Road of the Century," *Américas,* November, 1962, p. 2.

June, 1965, Castelo Branco announced a new schedule of government investment in an "initial" program for the development of the Amazon, to be used for water supply works, electric power plants, agricultural projects, and improved transportation. Shortly before the expiration of his term in office, the president established a SUDENE-like body to coordinate Amazonian development. Late in 1967, in a further attempt to spur regional economic growth, particularly through industrialization of products from the upper Amazon, Manaus was declared a free port.

Although much publicity has attended the launching of all these various valorization plans, there is little evidence that the funds spent thus far have brought about any significant social or economic changes, despite an occasional press release about the completion of a new road, health center, school, or small industry. If very much had been accomplished in the past 20 years, it is doubtful whether the introduction of two commercial crops by Japanese farmers and the opening of a single manganese mine would have attracted quite the attention they have received as economic landmarks. It remains to be seen whether the recent measures will have an effect that is any more marked than those that preceded them.

Even more than in the Northeast, the economic gap between the North and the more dynamic parts of the country has widened in recent years. For instance, during the last intercensal period, 1950 to 1960, the number of industrial establishments added throughout the entire North (578) was less than the increment in Sergipe alone (582); and the increase in the number of industrial workers in the North (3,747) was under the number added in Maranhão (4,491) during the same period. Although it differs from the Northeast in that its principal problem is under- rather than over-population, the North shares with that region the primary need for a revolutionary up-grading of its outmoded socio-economic structures. Only after that is accomplished can the North begin to tackle effectively the substantive problems of technology and development with which it is faced.

7   *The West*

T̲̲ͪₑ West includes 22 percent of Brazil's area, but only 4 percent of its population. It contains two states: Mato Grosso, about the size of Pará, 475,000 square miles; and Goiás, a little more than half as large at 250,000 square miles. Here too is the Federal District, which was established in 1955 and covers 2,244 square miles. As in the North, population densities are highest in the eastern part of this region: the two million plus people of Goiás average out to about 8 per square mile; Mato Grosso's one million inhabitants give the state an overall density of 2 persons per square mile, the same as that of the North. A comparison between Maps 4 and 6 shows there is also a south-to-north decreasing population gradient, with extremely low densities in the equatorial forest.

Some parts of the West are located within extensions of the Northern environment, and it resembles the North in being a vast, underdeveloped, underpopulated, and both physically and psycho-logically remote region of Brazil. But here the resemblance ends, as most of the West is in the Central Highlands at 1,000 to 4,000 feet elevation, and its landscape is typically one of endless stretches of dun-colored scrub savanna, interrupted by galleries of woodland along swales and valleys. Whereas in the North larger settlements are confined to the banks of the main rivers, in the West the princi-pal clusters of people are found along its few railroads and highways. To these the scattered farms and ranch headquarters in the valleys are linked by trails or poorly defined roads which criss-cross the flat, higher levels of the plateau.

SAVANNA AND FOREST

Most of the West is in the wet-dry tropics, with a fairly reliable alternation of humid equatorial and desert conditions (Chapter 1). If it were not for the latter situation, an average annual rainfall of 60 inches would be sufficient to support a tropical forest throughout. However, the length and intensity of the dry season in a region of deeply weathered and well-drained uplands creates a shortage of moisture except on lower lands where seepage provides year-round water from underground sources. Vegetation varies, therefore, according to the availability of ground moisture.

On the *chapadas,* or higher surfaces of the Central Highlands, which comprise the characteristic landform of the West, the exposure of the parent material to millions of years of chemical weathering has produced leached and impoverished soils that may be as much as sixty or more feet deep. The predominant vegetation on these lands is a mixture, in intricate and varied combinations, of tall tropical grasses and gnarled, stunted, semi-deciduous trees, or scrub. At first glance these savanna lands might seem ideal for mechanized farming as it is practiced in the grasslands of the temperate zone; but they are, in fact, totally unsuited for agriculture without the addition of large amounts of prohibitively expensive fertilizers. Even for cattle raising, which is virtually their only use, the carrying capacity is extremely low, and the coarseness and unpalatability of the grasses toward the end of the dry season reduce the herds to skin and bone.

While the grasses and scrub trees of the high peneplain surface turn sear and brown during the dry season, the valley bottoms remain perennially green, irrigated by subterranean water that fell on the plateau during the rainy period. In them the soils, derived from freshly weathered rock, are relatively shallow, young, and high in plant nutrients. The forests which grow there superficially resemble those of the equatorial region, but unlike the latter they add a significant quantity of organic matter to the soil because of the diminution of chemical and biological decomposition during the dry season. It is, therefore, only on these lower, mostly forested lands that farming takes place in the West (see, for example, Map 7).

RANCH AND FARM

Topography and soils assume primary importance in determining the agricultural patterns of the West because climatic conditions are fairly uniform throughout the region. Temperature variations due to elevation are, however, important in certain cases where specific crops are concerned. For instance, in these latitudes coffee growing starts at about 1,000 feet elevation, and wheat can only be grown above 2,400 feet. On the other hand, since the West is not subject to the degree of cold which characterizes the Andean plateaus or Brazil's Southern Plateau, temperate and sub-tropical crops may be grown side by side with bananas and other tropical plants.

Thanks to the great number of crops from which the farmers of the West may make a selection, farming varies considerably from place to place depending upon marketing conditions, traditions, and the preferences of individuals. The native of many generations usually supports himself by growing corn, cassava, and bananas on a small plot located in a valley, while on the savanna he grazes a herd of mestizo or Zebu (originally from India) cattle. In contrast to this static, near-subsistence farming that has traditionally been practiced in the West, variety is the cornerstone of a new, commercial agriculture. Newcomers from Minas Gerais or the Northeast also have their subsistence crops, but they grow commercial quantities of beans, dry rice, coffee, and sugar cane. Large coffee and cotton plantations generally belong to *Paulistas;* the Portuguese have a few olive groves; Japanese have revolutionized the local diet with their vegetable gardens; Italians run vineyards and apiaries; and some dairy herds graze in planted pastures, introduced by northern Europeans.

Commercial farming has evolved during the past two decades in the contiguous forested hill lands located in the southeastern districts of the West (Map 6). The three principal foci of such expansion are along the Paraná River in Mato Grosso, with outliers reaching to Campo Grande and Ponta Porã; in southern Goiás along the Paranaíba River; and in the south-central part of the same state, where the headwaters of the Tocantins and tributaries flowing toward the Paranaíba from the north have cut a "window" into the surrounding peneplain. Although population densities have been increasing steadily in recent years within each of these areas, the last-named, which is known as the *Mato Grosso de Goiás,* or Thick Goiás Forest, has received a truly impressive flood of immigrants.

This particularly high growth rate in the Mato Grosso de Goiás has come about due to a combination of favorable circumstances. First, there was a large extent of good agricultural land available that was either unowned or little valued by the region's large landowners, the cattlemen. Then, access to these lands was provided by an extension of the railway from Minas Gerais to Anápolis, at the rim of the forest, and later to Goiânia, in the Mato Grosso itself. The latter city was built in the late 1930's as the new state capital, and exerted a strong attraction in its own right. Finally, prospective settlers were swayed by the publicity which attended the success of the Federal Agricultural Colony on a tributary to the Tocantins, and by the assistance it offered them in their pioneer efforts to clear the virgin forest. Settlement of the Mato Grosso de Goiás, which now has one-third of the state's cultivated land, was in large measure responsible for doubling Goiás' population between 1950 and 1960 (whereas it had only increased by 25 percent during the preceding decade), and for increasing that state's share of Brazil's agricultural income from 2.9 to 3.5 percent since 1950.

Another region within the West that is worth special mention, albeit for different reasons, is the low-lying, periodically flooded Pantanal (see also Chapter 1). Too wet to support forest growth except for light woods on hummocks, levees, and the fringes of higher land, it superficially resembles the flooded grasslands of the Amazon. However, a long dry season with cooler temperatures favors the growth of more succulent grasses, whose nutrient value is augmented by fertile alluvial soils derived from nearby limestones and basalts. The traditional and almost exclusive activity in this region is cattle grazing, and four-fifths of the several hundred thousand head which are marketed in the East each year still reach their destinations by means of overland drives that may take from 60 to 90 days. The Pantanal *fazenda* is of the old style: it is huge, with perhaps several opulent ranch houses, and is staffed by a large band of faithful cowhands, almost a militia. The owner has enough money for the good things in life, and may go about his business or pleasure by private plane. The *fazendeiro's* sons receive a first-class higher education in Rio or São Paulo, although not many of the daughters are so favored as yet.

Among the still unused areas in the tropical world suited for agriculture, the Pantanal is potentially one of the most productive. It would need to be developed on the basis of a controlled water distribution system—an enormous task. The Pantanal's isolation from the rest of Brazil, its pattern of land ownership, and the traditional inclinations of its inhabitants, all make this a possibility only for the far distant future.

TRANSPORTATION AND DEVELOPMENT

The West, better than any other of Brazil's major regions, illustrates the fundamental role that land transportation plays in the development of so vast a country. It will be noted from Maps 3 and 4 that the highest population densities and largest settlements are concentrated in the southern and eastern parts of the West, which are the most accessible to the well-developed transportation networks of São Paulo and southern Minas Gerais. More specifically, the first and second cities of Goiás, Goiânia and Anápolis, with populations respectively of 130,000 and 50,000 (these were, it is of interest to note, 40,000 and 20,000 in 1950), are located at the two terminal points of the railroad to the south. Until very recently they were also on the only satisfactory road leading out of the state. The next five cities of Goiás by size, ranking third through seventh, are located toward the Paranaíba River, along either the road or the railroad. The state's eighth city is Formosa, not far from Brasília on the road from Anápolis to Bahia.

In Mato Grosso the functional relationship between lines of communication and settlement is just as clear. Along the narrow-gauge, wood-burning Noroeste do Brasil Railroad in the south, from east to west the following towns are listed in the last census: Três Lagoas, Mato Grosso's fourth city, with 15,000 inhabitants; Campo Grande, the largest, with 65,000; Aquidauana, fifth with 12,000; and Corumbá, the third largest with 43,000. At the end of a branch line to the south, Ponta Porã has 10,000 inhabitants and is in seventh place. On roads that lead east and west out of Ponta Porã are the state's sixth and ninth cities: Dourados, with 11,000 inhabitants, and Bela Vista with 9,000.

The only other significant east-west route across Mato Grosso is a 1,000-mile road from the Minas Triangle through the central part of the state. Only three cities are located along it. Rio Verde, near the Minas Gerais border, is in eighth place with 10,000 inhabitants. Cuiabá, the capital and second city of the state, has a population of 57,000. Cáceres, at the end of the road on the Paraguay River, with 8,000 people ranks tenth. Along these two transportation arteries, the road and the railroad, are Mato Grosso's ten largest settlements, as well as the complete roster of towns with over 5,000 population.

Two branches of the Rio Verde-Cáceres road lead northward: one to Diamantino, in the headwaters of the Paraguay River; the other to Barra das Garças and across the Araguaia to Goiás City, a small mining town that was formerly the state capital. Marking the northern limit of effective settlement on the equatorial forest borderland, these places are little more than hamlets in stagnant gold and diamond fields. Here, stranded prospectors eke out a meager existence panning worked-out placers and growing subsistence crops. Private land companies, notably one from Rio Grande do Sul, have begun colonization schemes on tracts along the forest rim in Mato Grosso. Although some of the few settlements there seem fairly successful, certain operators must be suspect because of the advertising they have aimed at non-resident foreigners, guaranteeing annual profits of 100 percent on plantation crops to be grown by tenant labor.

Despite some encouraging signs of growth during the past two decades, particularly in agriculture, the West has less than its proportional share of certain elements that are more and more becoming part of the economic structure of modern Brazil. The more important aspects of this are shown in Table 4, with figures from the last census. The most revealing figures are in the sets which can be used to compare the proportional number of industrial establishments with the relative value of their production. A majority of the plants, particularly in Mato Grosso, produce low value goods,

TABLE 4

The Western States—as Percentages of Brazilian Totals

	Goiás	Mato Grosso
Population	2.8	1.3
Gross Income	1.5	1.0
Income from Agriculture	3.4	2.1
Number of Industrial Establishments	1.4	1.0
Value of Industrial Production	0.4	0.3
Electric Power Consumption	0.4	0.2

involving the processing of raw materials from agriculture or for the most rudimentay aspects of the building trades, yielding modest returns on both investment and labor. It is interesting to note, in passing, that although in 1960 the West had nearly twice as many industrial establishments as did the North (2,697 plants versus 1,795), the value of its production was only about half that of the latter (3.8 billion *cruzeiros* as compared to 6.1 billion). It cannot be said, either, that the cause of this was the age of the West's physical plant, as two-thirds of those in operation had been built during the preceding decade (there were 1,067 in 1950). Most of the industrial "establishments" are, in fact, very small operations, employing four men on the average. They are frequently powered by mules, oxen, or old-fashioned water wheels—a situation that is not surprising considering the low level of electric power consumption within the region.

Such amenities as there are, are limited to the most favored areas and especially to the larger urban centers. At the other extreme, much of the West is still looked upon by Brazilians, not without reason, as the *sertão:* that ever-present wilderness which lies beyond the fringes of settlement and has been retreating westward ever since the first colonists moved back from the coast. In terms of its development, the West today includes the range from stone age villages, perhaps five thousand years behind current standards of progress; through cattle and mining communities 250 to 50 years removed in time; to towns and cities in various stages of twentieth-century evolution, up to the world's newest metropolis, Brasília.

In the north is a remote land of forest-clad valleys, sparsely peopled by primitive Indian tribes or lone hunters and prospectors. Official expeditions are still sent out to this part of the West to explore a river, lay a telegraph line, cut a trace for some future road building program, or simply to try to establish the Brazilian presence in the *sertão*. In the west and the center is a country of vast ranches, where cattle are raised in the traditional manner, the social structure is rigidly stratified, and politics are exclusively in the independent hands of the large landowners. In the southeast is the now well-established pioneer fringe, where new settlers have expanded farm-land and towns, giving to the area a dynamic spirit of individual enterprise unlike that found in any other part of the country. It is in this zone of change and optimism, not as is often claimed in an empty hinterland, that the new capital, Brasília, has been built: between modern industrial Brazil to the south and east and traditional rural Brazil to the north and west. The city lies, in every respect, mid-way between the nation's past and its future.

BRASÍLIA—SHOWPLACE OR HOLLOW SHELL?

Brasília did not spring full-blown out of the minds of a small clique of self-aggrandizing, somewhat lunatic politicians, as the unimaginative, the skeptical, and the reactionary members of the coastal oligarchy have led many to believe. The idea of moving the national capital into the interior occurred to some Brazilians over a hundred and fifty years ago, after the refugee Portuguese Court established itself in Rio. In 1891 an eventual transfer was written into the new Republican Constitution. In those heady and idealistic days, such a capital could be little more than a dream, as the *sertão* lay just beyond the second range of mountains, and Brazil's export-oriented, seaboard coffee economy had neither the reason nor the means for that kind of move. Even when the idea was revitalized during World War I and a survey was made of a site not far from the spot where Brasília now stands, the country had neither the population, the productivity, nor the necessary transportation into the interior to make the move a viable or even realistic one. When Juscelino Kubitschek ran for the Presidency in 1955, with the building of a new capital in the interior as one of the main planks in his platform, there were many who believed that these conditions still applied and that the time was not yet ripe. Even more people were convinced that Kubitschek's manifesto was just another vote-getting political gimmick, a promise to be forgotten once he had gained the office. But they failed to take into account his messianic enthusiasm for the project and his firm belief that this would both symbolize and stimulate the emergence of Brazil as a dynamic, modern nation.

In actual fact, a considerable amount of preliminary work had already been done before Kubitschek began his Presidential race. In the late 1940's a commission had studied the general question of which part of the country was most suitable for the location of a new capital. They decided upon an area about the size of Pennsylvania, designated the Federal Quadrilateral, which extended from the vicinity of Anápolis eastward across Goiás into Minas Gerais. Here transportation problems would not be too overwhelming, food was available from the pioneer farming area, and land values were not too high. From 1954 to mid-1955 a private consortium of mixed Brazilian and American technical personnel studied this quadrilateral, using the latest aerial photographic methods, and recommended five possible locations that would be suitable for a major city. Taking into consideration such matters as site, construction problems, water supply, transportation possibilities, and food and raw materials sources, another commission selected from among the five the actual spot upon which the capital was to be built. All these operations, ending in the delimitation of a Federal District, were conducted in utmost secrecy to avoid land speculation, and real estate transactions within the District were prohibited simultaneously with the public announcement of the definitive future location of Brasília. Parenthetically, some heated discussion also took place over the name, the traditionalists wanting to call it Santa Cruz, or in some versions Vera Cruz, the first Portuguese designation for the land that became Brazil. But they lost out because several cities and a Portuguese emigrant ship already bore that name, which made it seem something less than original.

In September, 1956, not long after assuming office, President Kubitschek created NOVACAP, the autonomous Company for the Urbanization of the New Capital, and gave it the job of building enough of the new city so that it could be inaugurated before the expiration of his term in 1961. Meanwhile, a competition had been held to determine the form Brasília was to take, and a contract for the design of the principal buildings was awarded to the winner, Lúcio Costa, and to Brazil's leading, world-famous architect, Oscar Niemeyer. NOVACAP personnel then erected their temporary canvas and wooden structures on the gently sloping, scrub-covered, and hitherto empty plateau from which the city was to rise. They had no sooner arrived than the holocaust of the rainy season was upon them. But the work began despite mud and the chill of driving rains and the need to overcome the incredible logistics of a thousand-mile road to the coast which, precarious at best, had turned into a quagmire.

A temporary airfield was finally completed, and the most desperately needed supplies could be flown in—not infrequently at lower overall cost than was possible using time-consuming and difficult surface transport. It was at this stage that opposition to

Brasília, which had sniped at and obstructed the work since its inception, reached a fever pitch, with accusations of waste and incompetence raging through the press. One ill-informed official even castigated NOVACAP for not using the magnificent Amazon waterway to bring in supplies, quite overlooking the fact that the nearest stream navigable even by canoe was probably hundreds of miles away through the jungle .

The common people of Brazil were not deceived by the prophets of doom, and they trekked by the thousands from all over the country to NOVACAP headquarters to take part in this great new venture. It is true that they were looking for jobs, or perhaps other, easier ways of making money. But everyone, whether laborer, storekeeper, or even official, brought with him or soon acquired the contagious spirit of the frontiersman. They settled in a garishly painted clapboard pioneer town (Map 7) officially called the *Nucleo Bandeirante,* but popularly known as the "Free City." Here one could relive the spirit of the Old West, although Jeeps replaced horses, and newcomers arrived by bus rather than by stagecoach. The Free City was soon larger than Anápolis, making it the second-largest city within the boundaries of Goiás. A strange collection of buildings, it included a barn-like church and a quonset hut movie theater, a large wooden bank beside a small shop selling Indian artifacts, hotels that looked like cottages and homes that were little more than huts, a restaurant specializing in boeuf strogonoff and crêpes suzettes, and prostitutes in tattered tents pitched on the edge of town. It was the people of this colorful town who moved the supplies, cleared the scrub, paved the roads, laid the airfield, built the dam, and raised a new metropolis brick-by-brick out of the wilderness. Today the Free City is only a collection of dilapidated shacks, and some day soon the government plans to bulldoze it out of existence. In its place will rise a monument to these latter-day *Bandeirantes* who, like their predecessors, hewed a dream out of the *sertão.* Meanwhile, a few *favelas* continue to exist, even in Brasília.

By mid-1958 the presidential "Palace of the Dawn" was completed, and some symbolic political events began to be held there. In rapid succession, from the dust rose the 28-story Congressional Office Building with its saucer-shaped satellites, the Senate Building and Chamber of Deputies; a cluster of huge, slab-like government office buildings, the glass sides of which shimmer like crystals under the sun's glare; and the austere yet graceful Supreme Court Building, with its seated figure of Justice, separated from the Presidential Office Building by a vast plaza holding a gigantic, open metalwork sculpture seemingly of two devil-gods in traditional Bahian folk style, but actually representing the workers who built Brasília, the *candangos*. As the months and years passed, the wings of the aeroplane-shaped city began to take form with shops, residential areas, a few preliminary embassy structures, and more and more of the neighborhood units known as Superblocks (*Superquadras*). And little by little the dusty avenues, laid out in cloverleaves and overpasses so there would be no crossroads, were paved. Grass and trees were planted on the bare soils of the *chapada*. The reservoir, Paranoã Lake above the hydroelectric dam, filled with water, and a yacht club arose on its banks. Brasília, which was inaugurated on April 21, 1960, before Kubitschek handed over the presidency, is today a functioning metropolis of some 300,000 inhabitants, including those living in its satellite towns. It is the largest city in the interior north and west of Belo Horizonte, only ten years after the first construction workers arrived on the scene.

It is true that there have been well founded criticisms of the Brasília project, especially of the haste with which the city was built. This led unavoidably to certain deficiencies in overall planning, as in the matter of getting people to and from work efficiently during the early stages of growth, and in actual construction, where flaws such as plaster peeling off new buildings are beginning to appear. Yet Kubitschek knew well that in the nature of Brazilian political maneuvering, if he did not present his successor with a *fait accompli,* the whole project and whatever had already been invested in it might well be abandoned. Subsequent chaotic political events seem to have vindicated his haste.

Other attacks revolved around the whole matter of moving the capital at all, particularly to so seemingly remote a location, when funds were needed for other phases of national development. Some of these objections can be dismissed as coming from people in the government who were loath to give up the easy life and the perquisites they had obtained for themselves in Rio. Others did not want to see vote-getting projects in their home constituencies abandoned. More legitimately, one must weigh the possible value to the country of other projects that had to be postponed against not only the enthusiasm and pride engendered by the symbol of Brasília, but also against the very tangible benefits it in fact did bring to the interior. Most important of these was the improvement of surface transportation, always one of the weakest links in the Brazilian economic chain. Existing roads were improved, such as the one from Rio to Belo Horizonte, which was mentioned in Chapter 4 as an important stimulus to industrial growth in the latter city; and new ones were built. The most spectacular and significant of these was the Bernardo Sayão Highway, named after the man who once headed the agricultural colony in the Mato Grosso de Goiás, had been Governor of Goiás, was one of the main people responsible for building Brasília, and died crushed beneath a tree on this road which he was in charge of constructing. Also known as the Belém-Brasília Highway, it sliced across a thousand and more miles of Amazonian rain forest and for the first time established overland connections between the central part of the country and the North, opening up hitherto uninhabited lands to a rush of colonization.

The mere presence of Brasília in the interior has done much to shrink the Brazilians' concept of distance, which at times has produced an almost traumatic hopelessness about ever bridging the gap between "civilization" and the *sertão*. As for criticism that the new capital is too remote, one might ask: too remote from what? The traditional enclaves of power on the coast? But one of the basic tenets in making the move was that it would break the stranglehold of an oligarchy headquartered in Rio whose personal economic and political interests were too often in conflict with the well-being of the nation. As, little by little, more Federal functions are transferred to Brasília with the aid of the physical and mental mobility of the air age [1] (Map 8), the national government should increasingly become the servant of all the people of Brazil, rather than of a privileged few. Although one cannot be so foolish as to expect miracles, there is no doubt that Brasília's impact will be felt long after its most vociferous critics have folded their beach umbrellas and departed from their accustomed places under the noonday sun at Copacabana.

[1] Brazil's largest airline, Varig, logs a thousand million passenger miles a year and, between its domestic and international flights, serves more cities than any other airline in the world.

8 *The Giant Stirs*

STANDING at the site upon which Brasília was to rise, President Kubitschek said, "From this solitude of the Central Plateau, shortly to be transformed into a center where vital national decisions will be made, I look toward tomorrow and foresee the dawn of my country's great destiny with unshakable faith and unlimited confidence." Toward the East and the South, that dawn was already lighting cities and farms. In the Northeast, fingers of light were spreading slowly over the countryside. Across the endless horizons of the Central Plateau and in the gloom of the Amazonian forest, a faint tinge of its illuminating rays was reflected in the night sky. Throughout this giant nation the people were stirring, preparing to deal confidently with a future that was already upon them.

In the traditional sense of the word, Brazil can no longer be considered an underdeveloped country. The world's fifth nation in area and eighth in population, it also stands eleventh in gross national product. Brazilian technicians have built atomic power plants and fired rockets into space. Contingents of Brazilian soldiers on United Nations missions help keep the peace in distant places. The national interest abroad is well cared for by the diplomats of *Itamarati,* Brazil's Foreign Service, long recognized as among the most distinguished and competent in the world.

ADAPTABILITY AND MODERATION,
CORNERSTONES OF PROGRESS

It is true that there are as yet vast reservoirs of untapped or under-utilized physical and human resources in Brazil, as the preceding chapters have shown in summary fashion. Much of this neglect is due to regional differences which have been accentuated by minimal contacts and lack of integration between the regions until recent years. Yet this very emptiness and diversity, in which each unit of the Republic has its own special backlog of unused space and skills, may ultimately prove to be among Brazil's greatest assets in an overcrowded, overused world. Improved communications and the beginnings of a modern scientific approach to resource utilization and regional integration represent the first steps toward as yet un-realized possibilities.

Any assessment of the national promise must certainly include the Brazilian people, with their great adaptability, their inventive flair, their humor, and their forebearance toward each other's dif-ferences and foibles, as well as those of strangers in their midst. Their unquenchable optimism is summed up by the national belief that "God is a Brazilian." This also expresses the universality of the Brazilian ethos, according to which social and regional sub-cultures are but easily bridged variants of the national whole. It is perhaps best illustrated in the matter of race relations, where the word "toleration," so common in more northern lands, plays no part, since the Brazilian simply sees nothing that particularly needs to be tolerated among his fellow citizens, especially anything that may be determined by so flimsy a criterion as skin color or bodily shape. This does not mean that racial awareness does not exist in Brazil. But classifications based upon it are not institutionalized and have no connotations of superiority or inferiority; they are exclu-sive rather than antagonistic, and they are founded primarily on traditional family or class prejudices, which are breaking down as society becomes more mobile and increasingly easy-going in matters of racial equality.

Classification by race in Brazil has no well-founded boundaries. It is entirely a subjective matter within the extremes of *Negro* (pure black), *Alemão* (literally German, applied to all fair skinned blonds), *Japonês* (for all Mongolians), or the true native *Índio*—all of which groups are diminishing as proportions of the general population. Most of the population falls loosely within the general class of *moreno,* a term which was originally applied to dark-skinned whites but has gradually been expanded to include many of those who might formerly have been considered *mulattos,* a term used in a more restricted sense in Brazil than is common in English-speaking countries. Some of the most famous *Bandeirantes,* as well as a number of the "coffee barons," belonged to this group. So have many public figures (including Nilo Peçanha, who was President from 1910 to 1914), military men, and members of the arts and professions. The feminine *morena* represents the ideal in Brazilian womanhood, as a random selection of carnival songs will substantiate. There is, furthermore, no "African," or Negro, subculture as such in Brazil, as African culture traits, like some derived from the Indian, have permeated to every member of the populace regardless of skin color. All are first, foremost, and solely "Brazilians."

Another quality which stands the Brazilians in good stead is the moderation, even skepticism, with which they view changes and crises such as would rock most other nations to their very foundations. Civil wars and rebellions, carried out with more journalistic than military fervor, have failed to generate ideological or sectional animosities which survived the termination of hostilities. The slaves were freed and an Emperor was overthrown with a minimum of fuss. Even the dictatorship was not a harsh one, and its shortcomings were openly discussed, criticized, and joked about with no fear of reprisal. Brazilians have brought to all their various political regimes a unique twist that has made them quite unlike their supposed counterparts elsewhere in the Western world. It has therefore often been difficult to distinguish one type of government from another.

The adaptability of Brazilian individuals and institutions in the face of seemingly drastic political changes is also reflected in their approach to economics, which appears to be based on an intuitive adjustment to the realities of the moment. Thus, the State Capitalism of Vargas' Estado Novo did not go much beyond the establishment of a few national industries in which private capital was allowed to participate. On the other hand, substantial nationalization was carried out during the ideologically uncommitted presidency of Juscelino Kubitschek. Goulart's regime, while ostensibly professing some form of Socialist democracy, kept one ear attuned to the wishes of the ranching and manufacturing oligarchy and never strayed far from acceptable standards of economic behavior. Finally, the military leadership which put Castelo Branco in power was quite happy to turn over to civilian experts its economic juggling act of trying to placate the workers, reform the agrarian structure, keep the businessmen happy, and establish Federal programs in areas needing government assistance. Doctrinaire approaches, whether of the Left or of the Right, have few proponents and a very small number of supporters, the whole matter being perhaps best summed up by the popular view that "Brazil progresses at night, while the politicians sleep."

THE GOVERNMENT'S ROLE IN THE ECONOMY

The government has, nevertheless, been playing an increasingly important role in the national economy over the past quarter of a century. This change has been gradual but necessary because of the shortage of private capital or the unwillingness of those who possess it to put it into productive use. Federal economic intervention has been carried out through a flexible combination of mixed corporations with both government and private shareholders, American T.V.A.-style programs, Soviet inspired "Five Year"-type plans, nationalization, and inflation.

The various "plans" and "programs," which have not been as far-reaching and inclusive as those established in many other countries, have served primarily to give direction to regional or national development schemes, which have been discussed in other chapters.

Some limited nationalization has taken place as a matter of necessity, rather than for doctrinaire reasons. Expropriations, characteristically with adequate compensation, have included a small amount of private land, certain public services, most of the shipping, and the railways. In virtually every case the owners, frequently foreign, had been operating the expropriated facilities at levels detrimental to public or national needs, in order to maximize profits.

Among the numerous examples of government entry or partial entry into business ventures, two of the most significant are the Volta Redonda steel mill and the F.N.M. (National Motor Factory) motor vehicle plant. Both represented pioneering steps in industries requiring large investments, and paved the way for later investments of private capital in these basic industries. On the other hand, *Petrobras,* the state-run petroleum corporation with a monopoly on crude oil extraction in Brazil, was established by Vargas for nationalistic reasons at a time when American economic colonialism still flourished openly in Latin America, because of the fear that foreign companies would exploit the country's natural resources and deplete them against future needs. Subject in its infancy to bungling and mismanagement not unrelated to its use as a source of political patronage, *Petrobras* now supplies half the national consumption of crude oil, and the country is expected to become self-sufficient with the development of new deposits in Maranhão. In April, 1966, *Petrobras* took delivery of the first oil tanker ever made in a Brazilian shipyard. It would seem that, in general, direct government participation in the economy has had a salutary effect, acting as a stimulus to further growth.

The most subtle yet most far-reaching form of the government's intervention in the Brazilian economy has been its reliance upon inflation to finance economic expansion and to pay for some of its day-to-day operations. The need for an inflationary policy was created by the fact that private savings were seldom used for constructive purposes and that the government was unable to collect more than a fraction of the taxes it was theoretically owed. To fill this gap, the government took to the printing presses for the extra money it needed, thereby extracting each year a certain proportion of the value of the money which passed through or was held in private hands. Thanks to the usual Brazilian sense of moderation, inflation has generally been kept within tolerable limits and is accepted as a normal functioning of the economy.

During the 1940's the average inflationary rate was 15 percent *per annum,* rising to 20 percent from 1950 through 1958. The average for the next four years, which coincided with the costly construction of Brasília and an expanded road building program, was 50 percent per year. During Goulart's presidency matters got out of hand, as the rate of inflation averaged 90 percent *per annum* during 1963 and 1964, and was spiraling steadily upward, even though he had very little to show for this high rate besides an inflated bureaucracy. Under Goulart the annual increase in public expenditures rose from an average rate of 18 percent during the preceding 15 years to 30 percent in 1963 and 1964; but the increase in the gross national product dropped to only 1.4 percent a year. In contrast, during the two decades preceding 1963 the G.N.P. had been growing at an average rate of 5.8 percent a year, and capital formation averaged 17 percent, both adjusted for inflation (much higher growth rates, incidentally, than those of many Latin American countries whose currencies were stable). With a population growth that averaged about 3 percent, the greatly reduced increment of productivity in 1963–64 meant a net per capita decline of 1.8 percent *per annum* in the G.N.P. These events, rather than his doctrinaire pronouncements or political bungling, were the basic reasons for Goulart's ultimate downfall.

Castelo Branco's program to reduce inflation (Chapter 2), although disappointing to those expecting its disappearance despite the nature of Brazil's economic history, brought it back to a near normal rate of 45 percent *per annum;* and in 1965 the G.N.P. rose by 7.3 percent, about the same rate as in 1961. Thus, the country's economy was clearly in better shape than the alarmists had been willing to admit. Although one may decry the effects of inflation upon the wage-earning sectors of the Brazilian population, it has undoubtedly been a positive force in the growth of that nation. Furthermore, other methods of forcing savings and postponing consumption, whether under the early capitalism of Europe and the United States or the planned dislocations of Communism, have achieved industrial growth only by imposing far greater sacrifices and hardships on the laboring classes than those imposed in Brazil during the past quarter of a century.

A QUARTER CENTURY OF GROWTH

During the last twenty-five years Brazil has managed to overcome, if not profit by, changes brought about by unsettled political conditions and social dislocations. These have been associated with a tremendous population growth (from 41 million in 1940 to today's 85 million); the accelerated pace of urbanization, which has produced some 40 million city dwellers at the present time compared to only 13 million in 1940; and the shift from a rural toward an industrial economy. From the late 1940's to 1965 agriculture's share of the national income dropped from 39 to 23 percent while industry's share rose from 21 to 33 percent. Or, put in another way, from a 1949 base of 100, the index of real industrial production rose to 336 by 1965 while that of agriculture increased only to 223, although the latter retained a comfortable margin over population growth, which had an index figure of 170 for the same period.

Throughout this past quarter of a century the nation has exhibited sound economic growth. Even during the unsettled period from 1960 through 1965, Brazil's G.N.P. increased at an average annual rate of 4.9 percent, consumption rose at a rate of 4.3 percent, and per capita productivity went up by about 4 percent a year. Furthermore, the development of a high level of industrial and technical competence and output has been having an increasing impact. By the 1960–65 quinquennium it was possible to reduce imports by an average of 9 percent a year. Now only 0.5 percent of Brazil's durable consumers' goods needs must be met by imports, and the country can supply about 70 percent of the national requirements for heavy industrial equipment from internal sources.

The principal, but by no means insoluble, problem remaining in Brazil's foreign trade pattern is its reliance on external sources for about one-half of its crude oil and wheat needs, which between them account for one-third of the total value of imports.

During the 1960's Brazil was able to increase its exports at an average annual rate of 3.1 percent. In 1965 and 1966 the country showed trade surpluses on the order of $500 million, with a record $1.8 billion in exports in the latter year (preliminary figures at press time indicate that the 1967 balance may be less favorable due to increased imports and lower export prices). More important has been Brazil's growing emphasis on industrial exports, which showed a yearly increase of 60 percent during 1965 and 1966. In 1965 manufactures overtook cotton and ores (iron and manganese) to rank second by value in the list of exports, after coffee. This does not mean that agricultural exports have declined absolutely, as Brazil continues to supply half the world's coffee (production is about 30 million bags a year, of which some 17 million are exported) and has a significant share of the world market in cotton, cocoa, sisal, rice, tobacco, bananas, corn, and black pepper. In 1966 Brazil even began exporting strawberries—to Florida!

Brazil's list of industrial exports is as diverse as that of its farm produce. Included, for example, are motor vehicles and parts, diesel engines, sewing machines, household appliances, cutlery, and business machines, to name only a few. The products which were exported for the first time in 1965 show an interesting variety, ranging from steel and synthetic rubber, to cigarette manufacturing machinery and elevators, to earth moving equipment and microscopes. In 1966 Brazil sent the largest rock crusher ever made in Latin America to Argentina; began exporting tractors, which it only started producing in 1960; and received an order from Mexico for ships worth US $27.5 million, the largest industrial transaction ever made within the Latin American Free Trade Association. Recently machinery for manufacturing incandescent lamps was sent to the United States—and a line of Brazilian bathing suits was exported to California. Brazil also boasts the only company in the world outside the U.S. which is licensed by the Federal Aviation Authority to manufacture motor parts for American commercial aircraft.

This industrial development has attracted and thrived on foreign capital, which at present is estimated to amount to between $3.5 and $4 billion, compared to $1 billion in 1951. About 40 percent of all foreign investments have come from the United States, going primarily into manufacturing, rather than into extractive industries as American interests have elsewhere in Latin America. Brazil has also received more capital from Sweden, West Germany, and Japan than these nations have invested in any other foreign country.

Foreign investments entering Brazil declined to about $30 million in 1962 and 1963 and to only $5 million in 1964. However, by 1965 the inflow of private money from abroad was back up to $257 million, just slightly less than in the peak year of 1961. Recently, a foreign investment guarantee treaty was signed between Brazil and the United States which entitles American investors to insurance against such risks as war, expropriation, or currency inconvertibility. A similar agreement is being worked out with West Germany. Renewed international confidence in Brazil's economic promise and future stability is shown by the fact that after Castelo Branco came to power, loans and credits were advanced by the U.S.S.R., the Export-Import Bank of Japan, the World Bank, and the Inter-American Development Bank, the latter having virtually ignored Brazil during the Goulart regime.

BRAZIL'S ROLE IN THE MODERN WORLD

Today Brazil can hardly be characterized as an "underdeveloped" country, despite the vast areas within it that await development. It would be even less appropriate to classify it among the "banana republics," as Brazil has always been able to maintain a healthy degree of independence from American intervention in its affairs by virtue of its size, remoteness, and self-sufficiency. On the other hand, because Brazil has not been forced by feelings of inferiority to automatically denounce the "Colossus of the North" at every turn, she has been able to side with the United States when it was in her interest to do so. In general, Brazil has proved to be a loyal, if by no means uncritical, ally of the United States. She sent an expeditionary force to Italy during World War II; supplied the commanding general and numerous troops to the Organization of American States' "police" force in the Dominican Republic; and late in 1966 intercepted a U.S.S.R. ship bound for Cuba with an embargoed cargo. On the other hand, Brazil recently withheld her support from a proposed Inter-American Peace Force (aimed largely at Castroite machinations on the continent, it was strongly backed by the U.S.) and also from a Latin American nuclear non-proliferation treaty until her right to carry out "peaceful" atomic explosions was recognized.

It is noteworthy that Brazil's alternating positions on Cuba and other matters of not inconsiderable regional, and even international, significance have brought no reprisals from either Communism or the West, which emphasizes that country's sufficient strength to formulate its own foreign policy. Because of this independence, a usually pragmatic and non-doctrinaire approach to international affairs, and a history of unaggressive relations with her neighbors (if one excepts the annexation of Acre from Bolivia after the area's *de facto* occupation by Brazilian rubber gatherers), Brazil has emerged as the leader of Latin America, despite Argentine and Mexican bids for this role among the smaller Hispanic nations.

On a wider scale, Brazil is becoming a model for emergent nations. Some of the reasons for this new role are the successful handling of both internal and external affairs by avoiding the extremes of Left or Right, racial harmony, a dynamic economy, and peaceful relations with other countries. No nation of comparable size and population has compiled as enviable a record of international friendship as has Brazil. In a world where these qualities have all too often been lacking, Brazil's sense of moderation and tolerance, combined with steady social and economic evolution, offer meaningful examples to those nations that make up what the

French are pleased to call *Le Tiers Monde*. And Brazil's leadership is, indeed, by example, rather than by the strident, messianic professions of superiority which characterize so many of the self-proclaimed leaders of today's world. Ideally, Brazil will move others to emulation, as she bestirs herself toward an enviable future.

A Selected Glossary of Brazilian Terms Used in the Text

agreste—light woodland of the Northeast

Araucaria—Paraná Pine, *Araucaria angustifolia*

Bandeirante—member of a migratory band of explorers, especially from São Paulo but also from the Northeast, known as a Bandeira

bombilla—hollow metal spoon for sipping mate

caatinga—thorn scrub of the Northeast

caboclo—in the narrow sense a person of mixed white and Indian blood, but more widely used to denote a backwoodsman or rustic

caiçara—coastal fisherman using primitive techniques

caipira—hillbilly

candango—workers who came, mostly from the Northeast, to build Brasília

Capichaba—native of Espírito Santo State

Capitanía—early colonial territorial administrative division

Carioca—native of the city of Rio de Janeiro

chapada—high, nearly level surface of the Central Plateau

coronéis—(pl. of coronél, lit. colonel) large landowners and political bosses

cruzeiro—Brazilian currency replacing the former mil réis unit

estancia—large ranch in Rio Grande do Sul

favela—shantytown

favelado—person living in a favela

fazenda—large ranch or plantation

fazendeiro—owner of a large ranch or plantation

flagelado—refugee from a natural calamity

friagem—cold wave

garimpeiro—prospector

gaucho—Rio Grande do Sul cowboy, also a native of that state

Itamarati—from Itamarati Palace, where the Foreign Office is located in Rio de Janeiro, now synonymous with that department of the Brazilian government

lotação (pl. lotações)—mini-busses

Maranhaense—native of Maranhão State

mate—South American indigenous tea

mil réis—lit. one thousand reals, former unit of currency replaced by the cruzeiro

Mineiro—native of Minas Gerais State

Nordestino—native of Northeastern Brazil

135

patrão—boss, applied to a landowner or the owner of a business by those working
    there
Paulista—native of São Paulo State or city
seringueiro—rubber gatherer in the Amazon
sertão—backlands or wilderness
sesmaria—colonial land grant to an individual
tabuleiro—low coastal plateau
terra-firme—land in the Amazon Valley not subject to seasonal flooding
terra roxa—reddish-purple soils derived from basalt
várzea—that part of the Amazon floodplain subject to seasonal flooding
vaqueiro—cowboy

Recommended Further
Readings on Brazil

Jorge Amado, *Gabriela, Clove and Cinnamon,* Knopf, 1962.

Aroldo de Azevedo, editor, *Brasil, a Terra e o Homem* (3 vols.), Cia. Editora Nacional (São Paulo), 1964.

Edouard Bailby, *Brésil, Pays Clef du Tiers Monde,* Calmann-Lévy (Paris), 1964.

Erik Baklanoff, editor, *New Perspectives of Brazil,* Vanderbilt University Press, 1966.

Brazilian Embassy, *Survey of the Brazilian Economy, 1965,* Washington, 1967.

Euclydes da Cunha, *Rebellion in the Backlands,* Chicago University Press, 1944.

Gilberto Freyre, *The Masters and the Slaves,* Widenfeld & Nicolson (London), 1956.

———, *New World in the Tropics,* Knopf, 1959.

Celso Furtado, *The Economic Growth of Brazil,* University of California Press, 1963.

———, *Diagnosis of the Brazilian Crisis,* University of California Press, 1965.

Irving Louis Horowitz, *Revolution in Brazil,* Dutton, 1964.

Carolina Maria de Jesus, *Child of the Dark,* Signet Books, 1962.

Claude Lévi-Strauss, *Tristes Tropiques* (trans. John Russell), Criterion, 1961.

Richard P. Momsen, Jr., *Routes over the Serra do Mar,* Ball State University Bookstore (Muncie, Indiana), 1964.

John dos Pasos, *Brazil on the Move,* Doubleday, 1963.

Wm. Lytle Schurz, *Brazil the Infinite Country,* Dutton, 1961.

T. Lynn Smith, *Brazil, People and Institutions,* Louisiana State University Press, 1963.

Willy Stäubli, *Brasilia,* Leonard Hill Books (London), 1966.

Charles Wagley, *Amazon Town: A Study of Man in the Tropics,* Macmillan, 1953.

————, *An Introduction to Brazil,* Columbia University Press, 1963.

Index